Rocking the Boat

Academic Women and Academic Processes

Edited by

Gloria DeSole and Leonore Hoffmann

for the

Commission on the Status of Women in the Profession

The Modern Language Association of America

NEW YORK 1981

Copyright © 1981 by The Modern Language Association

Library of Congress Cataloging in Publication Data
Main entry under title:

Rocking the boat.

Bibliography: p.
1. Women College teachers—United States—
Addresses, essays, lectures. 2. Language teachers
—United States—Addresses, essays, lectures.
3. Modern Language Association of America—Addresses,
essays, lectures. I. DeSole, Gloria, 1937–
II. Hoffmann, Leonore, 1929–   III. Modern
Language Association of America. Commission on
the Status of Women in the Profession.
LB2332.3.R62   378'.12'088042   81-14030
ISBN 0-87352-330-X (pbk.)   AACR2

Published by The Modern Language Association of
America, 62 Fifth Avenue, New York, New York 10011

Cover design by Margaret Boys-Stone.

Contents

CONTENTS

Introduction

Rocking the Boat: Academic Women and Academic Processes is the fourth publication in a series sponsored by the Commission on the Status of Women in the Profession of the Modern Language Association. This series attempts to describe the concerns of women faculty and then to propose remedies. Like the first three (*Academic Women, Sex Discrimination, and the Law; "Unladylike and Unprofessional": Academic Women and Academic Unions*; and *Careers and Couples: An Academic Question*), this volume evolved from vigorous discussion at MLA conventions. We thought that a collection of essays detailing the experiences of women who chose to fight the negative decisions of academic institutions on questions of appointment, equal pay, tenure, and promotion would be of value to the profession.

When we conceived *Rocking the Boat*, we were both engaged in legal actions against our academic institutions. As members of the Commission on the Status of Women in the Profession, we were aware that our situations were not unusual. Since that time, four years have passed. One of us lost her suit; the other is still waiting for a finding from a state division for human rights. We have learned that such losses and delays are common.

We invited essays on academic grievances. Some essays arrived quickly; others came much later. One contributor wrote to us: "What a difficult process it was to go through the whole thing again in my head. I hadn't realized I'd feel it again that keenly." And that contributor, Carole Rosenthal, had won her case. Others who promised essays discovered that it was just too painful for them to review and record what they had discovered about their profession, their institutions, and themselves. But Rosenthal said that writing the essay was, finally, "cathartic." She continued, "I'd like to pass on what I gained from that experience to other women."

As we read the papers and listened to women talk about their situations, the scope of *Rocking the Boat* widened. We had imagined detailed factual accounts of why and how academic women pursued grievances within institutions and through state and federal agencies and courts. Such accounts do make up a large part of this collection. Many women, however, wanted to share their perceptions and their analyses of those perceptions. They had come to believe that women as women are viewed as interlopers on that great and stately ship, the *Academy*, as it sails the ocean of learning. It had come to seem that no matter what research women do, how well we teach, what color we are, whether we are single or married, lesbian or heterosexual, beautiful or plain, we are not welcome on board. No matter how egalitarian the institutional rhetoric, women as a group are seen as outsiders. For many that realization has brought home a painful but valuable insight. We need not feel that we have brought the rejection upon ourselves. It seems that we only presume to careers as teachers and scholars, and the institutions in which we work remind us in a variety of ways of our presumption. Many of these essays record the shock of recognition that the writers experienced as they perceived that established academics value women as students but not as colleagues. Apparently we may sit and learn but not stand and teach, or at least not stand and teach with tenure and in the upper ranks in the universities that awarded us our degrees.

Data collected early in the 1970s in studies like the commission's own *Study III: Women in Modern Language Departments, 1972–73* showed that academic women most often work in two- and four-year colleges. When we are present in universities, most of us are lecturers or assistant professors. And in the current financial climate whatever gains we have made are in jeopardy, for our chances, like those of our new male colleagues, of being dismissed at tenure time are excellent. Or if, against the odds, we are awarded permanent appointment, we are expected, as one writer puts it, to be "absurdly grateful" and then silent.

The same dismal picture remains as the new decade proceeds. The *Carnegie Quarterly* titled its 1973 survey "Making Haste Slowly: The Outlook for Women in Higher Education."[1] WOMEN FACULTY LOSE A LITTLE GROUND, NCES REPORTS was the headline in the *Higher Education Daily* in February 1976.[2] "Change without progress" is the summary statement in 1978 on women's status on college campuses since 1970 of Marjorie Bell Chambers, president of the American Association of University Women.[3] Behind those phrases is the recurring pattern of women faculty discriminated against in hiring and promotion, paid less than men for doing the same work, more likely to be given undergraduate classes and heavier loads, and finally less likely than male colleagues to receive tenure. "The documentation available," according to one book-length study, "constitutes clear presumptive evidence that the low status of women in higher education is due to discriminatory attitudes and action by male academics."[4]

Of course, the academy itself is not expanding; fewer men as well as women are being hired and tenured (Fishel & Pottker, p. 12). Nevertheless, the 1978 Women's Equity Action League report *Facts on Women in Higher Education* concludes: "What we have in the final analysis is a core group of exceptionally well-motivated and well-qualified women. The question is, do they have equal access to available jobs? The answer is no."[5]

Unfortunately, as a new decade begins, many academics, both male and female, believe otherwise. Expanding federal legislation and increasing discussion of affirmative action have created an illusion of progress. This illusion is responsible for the premature optimism about the status of women in higher education prevalent among many men and some women (Fields, p. 14). According to the WEAL report these are the facts:

- *Employment.* In all but a couple of fields women with doctorates have a higher unemployment rate than do men with doctorates.
- *Rank.* During the last several years the percentage of women faculty at all levels and in all kinds of institutions has increased only slightly. Women are still clustered in the lower ranks. Four times as many men as women are promoted to full professor.
- *Salary.* Women are more likely to be found at two-year institutions, where salaries are lower, than at four-year institutions with graduate schools. Women earn less than men for both nine- and twelve-month contracts from the rank of lecturer to professor.

According to the annual report of the American Association of University Professors, the weighted average salary for women as a percentage of the average salary for men for all ranks in all institutions (except those without rank) was 79.9 for 1978–79.[6]

Antidiscrimination laws have been on the books for years now. Title IX of the Education Amendments of 1972 forbids discrimination on the basis of sex in federally assisted educational programs. Yet "paper compliance," a show of attention by the college or university, remains the only solid evidence of "change." According to Chambers, Title IX "remains the unenforced law of this land" (Fields, p. 14). Suzanne Howard, assistant director for education programs of the AAUW, has concluded that work done by women does not carry the same value as that performed by men.[7] College administrators answering a survey that the AAUW conducted at six hundred four-year colleges indicated that "antagonistic attitudes within the university community still are the most significant obstacle to equity for women" (Fields, p. 14). Of course the antagonism, both individual and institutional, is usually covert. Since the prevalent belief is that women are making rapid progress, or that they may even have an edge, the woman who senses a lack of support for her teaching and scholarship and even for her presence in the academy is likely to blame herself. In the first part of this volume, as many of the women describe their passage through the academic processes, they record the difference between what they have been told about academic due process and what they experience for themselves. The reader can see these women's disorientation changing to outrage and then to a flow of energy that helps them fight the inequity, and finally to a sorrow that such a battle is necessary.

The essays in Part I, "Case Histories," recount individual women's struggles for equitable treatment within the available academic and governmental processes. These case histories also chronicle the writers' efforts to comprehend the academy in which such decisions are made. The struggle to comprehend often comes down to the bitter question, Is this whole system organized to exclude me?

Part II, "Contexts and Processes," includes four pieces of another sort. Three of them raise issues that demonstrate the obstructions and complications that beset those who want to open the world of higher education to full and fair participation of women. The final essay suggests a strategy that offers some support to the individual in this long struggle for equity.

It would be possible, perhaps even comfortable, to find the authors of these essays melodramatic and self-serving. The questions they raise about the university do not permit us to consider higher education in its familiar guise as the seat of benign authority and eternal truth. It would be convenient here, too, to dismiss the victims as unprofessional or unscholarly and to find their essays em-barrassing. The alternative is to recognize that the institutions of higher education are a part of contemporary society, for better or for worse. They are not above the biases of the culture and should not be above the laws of the land.

In March 1980 a federal court of appeals made the first tentative award of tenure in a decision supporting a woman faculty member's claim of sex discrimination. The court rejected the institution's response that such a finding would infringe on academic freedom:

> "The fact that the discrimination in this case took place in an academic rather than commercial setting does not permit the court to abdicate its responsibility to insure the award of a meaningful remedy," the Third Circuit said. Congress did not

intend that those institutions which employ persons who work primarily with their mental faculties should enjoy a different status [under federal antidiscrimination laws] than those which employ persons who work primarily with their hands.[8]

The ideas that the academy is value-free, pure, and thus, in practice, at least, above the law may seem absurd when so badly put, but it remains implicit in the typical defense of institutions as they argue against the interference of the courts in their internal employment decisions.

Of course many who value the institutions of higher education would hold them to the highest standard. If the writers in this collection had not shared that view, they would not have responded so strongly to what they saw as their institutions' failure to live up to that standard that their lives were changed as a result of their challenges to the academy. This volume does not presume to judge the merits of these writers' individual cases. Nor does it strive for a balanced response. It intends to give women who have rocked the boat some opportunity to speak out. Those who speak for "business as usual" in higher education have long had the platform almost entirely to themselves. The editors, however, do not wish to simplify the issues so that all academic women appear good and strong and right while all academic men are portrayed as knaves or fools. Some women, like some men, are incompetent and unqualified for jobs and promotions. Indeed, as the economy falters many male faculty are finding it difficult to remain in higher education. In these lean years, anguish about one's academic career is not restricted to women. Nevertheless, academic women face a systemic and individual prejudice. That systemic prejudice is what we mean when we speak of sex discrimination in higher education. *Rocking the Boat* is intended to illuminate some of the effects of that discrimination.

One academic woman, invited to read these essays in manuscript, has summarized what we hope is the intent, message, and value of *Rocking the Boat*.

> Generally, this book falls somewhere between the action handbook and the documentary, and its remarkable range of sensibility and experiences serves only to underscore the unanimity of its conclusion: academic women can place little confidence in the machineries of academic process where questions of their own tenure and promotion are concerned, and resorting to the extramural protection of the law, government agencies, and the courts is more often than not a long-term

experience, financially and psychologically harrowing, whose outcome is problematical at best. . . .

Is the book anything more than an anguished, collective *cri de coeur* from a group of academically "jilted" women? Will the profession at large be educated and urged toward corrective insight and action? Will women in the profession find the book helpful in constructing a professional consciousness about their own options, their assets and liabilities as women in a male-dominated [field]? Will the individual and collective presence and worth of women in the profession be affirmed and enhanced for all readers—men and women alike—by the publication of this book? I think the answer to these four questions is an unequivocal yes.

Indeed, one . . . aspect of this book is the amazingly affirmative, humane, and curative moral impulse that almost invariably attends the recitation of grievous outrages in narrative after narrative. There is nothing naive about this generous impulse. It exists in the . . . presence of radical awareness of inequity, bias, illegality, and immorality. And still the women affirm themselves, one another, and the meaning of that work of teaching and research to which they have committed themselves—often against impossible cultural odds. In so affirming, . . . the individual and collective voices here achieve genuine prophetic stature.

This book has, in my opinion, more than practical value, though I do not mean to derogate the practical value for any individual reader of seeing exactly what any number of academic women have gone through in their attempt to gain equal employment opportunity and how they have attempted—and sometimes achieved—remediation of wrongs. But, in addition to its practical value as a due-process manual, this book also stands at the cutting edge of some profound pedagogical and philosophical questions. What is it in the man-made academic world that needs—almost beyond individual impulse—to reject what it perceives to be woman as woman? What way exists out of the labyrinthine myth of "male expertise" when courts themselves refer questions of judgment back to the all-male academic establishment whose judgment, in fact, is the challenged entity? And what does our culture learn when it "goes to school" under such psychointellectual conditions?

The post-Hemingway grace under pressure represented by these essayists documents in an extraordinarily humane way what it is that women have to bring to the academy beyond mere competence in their specialization. These women have faced concerted and widespread bias and have responded to it with *caritas*, to use essayist Kantrowitz's culminating term. Together these essays offer a strongly sanative and morally restorative center. That moral center, variously articulated but ever present, makes this book a unified text and not merely an ad hoc collection.

These essays raise many issues. What do we as women do to sabotage ourselves? How can we be the allies of other academic women? And again and again the crucial question arises: Is the effort to remain an academic worth the agony? This volume, despite some hopeful pages, accumulates some discouraging evidence. In essay after essay, higher education is demonstrated to be replete, as Carole Rosenthal says, "with a sexism that is so basic, so casual, so overriding that it was almost out of consciousness."

In her poem "Translations," Andrienne Rich was writing about love, not about sexism in higher education; yet her last line—"this way of grief is shared, unnecessary and political"—is true here, too. To a woman, the writers in this volume write about their grief, about all our grievances, as "shared, unnecessary, and political." We are, however, in the early stages of a massive social change. We know that the affirmative action statements of the academy are at best statements of goals, not descriptions of realities. We must not feel failure prematurely. Instead, we must learn from the experiences of our colleagues.

Gloria DeSole
Leonore Hoffmann

NOTES

[1]"Making Haste Slowly: The Outlook for Women in Higher Education," *Carnegie Quarterly*, 21 (Fall 1973), 50.

[2]"Women Faculty Lose a Little Ground, NCES Reports," *Higher Education Daily*, 2 Feb. 1976, pp. 3–5.

[3]Quoted in Cheryl M. Fields, "'Change without Progress' for Women on Campus," *Chronicle of Higher Education*, 17 Apr. 1978, p. 14.

[4]Andrew Fishel and Janice Pottker, *National Politics and Sex Discrimination in Education* (Lexington, Mass.: D.C. Heath, 1977), p. 12.

[5]*Facts on Women in Higher Education* (Washington, D.C.: WEAL, 1977).

[6]"An Era of Continuing Decline: Annual Report on the Economic Status of the Profession, 1978–79," *Academe: Bulletin of the AAUP*, Sept. 1979, p. 17.

[7]"Women Faculty Members Earn Less Than Men, NCES Study Shows," *Equal Opportunities in Higher Education*, 18 Dec. 1978, p. 8.

[8]"Appeals Court Upholds Tenure Award in Bias Case," *Equal Opportunities in Higher Education*, 10 Mar. 1980, p. 5.

Part I

CASE HISTORIES

The Most Important Thing for You to Know

Marcia R. Lieberman

The most important thing for you to know is this: They will try to persuade you that you are being denied tenure (or promotion, or reappointment) because of your deficiencies. The argument most certain to take you in is the one that speaks to your self-doubt, so they will tell you that your publications are mediocre, your teaching weak. Don't believe it.

Discrimination against women may be the last form of bias that remains socially acceptable in this country. Sexist jokes, for example, are still tolerated where racist jokes are avoided, and there are many who still think it appropriate or "natural" that women should occupy a different place and move at a different pace (and in a different style) than do men. Exploration of the reasons for this attitude lies beyond the scope of this essay. Sexism is also one of the last forms of discrimination to remain lawful. Laws have protected academic women only since 1972, when Title VII of the Civil Rights Act of 1964 became applicable to college and university personnel.

Women face two forms of discrimination: open and covert. For many years injustice toward members of various minority groups was open in this country; it was lawful and socially acceptable. It incurs no penalties and brings no shame. For example, in 1969, when discrimination against women was more open, a senior colleague told me over lunch at the faculty club that I would have to be twice as good as a man to hold my job. There have been times in this country when segregation and exclusion were openly practiced: Cabinet members who were overheard telling racist jokes have not always had to resign.

When a person is denied something because of open discrimination practiced as a policy, that person's qualifications are never the question. What is excluded is a class, and thus all members of that class are excluded, whatever their qualifications or merits. When black people were not permitted to eat at lunch counters, each one was excluded regardless of whether he or she had enough money to buy a lunch. When the individual's qualifications are not the issue, there is no pretense of equity. Blacks are excluded because they are black, Jews because they are Jewish, women because they are female.

When discrimination is declared unlawful, other dangers can arise for affected classes. Intolerance made illegal goes underground, becomes covert and thus treacherous as well as unjust. Now pretext enters. Discrimination is denied and actions that result from discrimination are held to be caused by the person or class discriminated against. No one will admit to practicing discrimination; therefore, either it does not exist or it exists but cannot be "proved."

Opponents of affirmative action tend to deny that discrimination has been practiced against women as a class. They assert that universities are and have always been "gender-blind." (Most universities now declare themselves in writing to be equal opportunity employers.) If evidence is produced to show that academic women are awarded tenure and promotion less often than academic men and that they are clustered in less prestigious institutions as well as at lower academic ranks, opponents of affirmative action respond that the fault lies with the women themselves: they preferred teaching to research, did not publish, spent time raising children, were less than serious about their careers. Affirmative action consists of many elements, but its opponents claim that there is only one: hiring at the entry level. They agree that a qualified woman should be hired—if one should ever appear. To this end, they propose that women should be trained, so that eventually there will be a pool of qualified women from which to hire. But they ignore or reject other components of affirmative action, those that deal with the treatment of women further up the academic ladder, women who are up for reappointment, promotion, or tenure or women who are seeking new positions in mid-career. Yet affirmative action has to do with retention as well as with entry-level hiring; otherwise it simply perpetuates the revolving-door pattern. (During the trial of my tenure case, one of the university's lawyers objected to the introduction of a U.S. Department of Health, Education and Welfare report that found evidence of discrimination against faculty women at all ranks at the university. The HEW report, he argued, had nothing to do with my case; all it said was that the university ought to hire more women.)

The consequences of covert discrimination for women as a class and as individuals are similar. In order to avoid the penalties of the law, those who practice discrimination covertly must rally their forces and make a concerted effort to prove that the woman, a potential complainant, is inadequate. The insidious aspect of covert discrimination is that it seeks to persuade the victim that she is to blame for her predicament. Besides depriving its victims of such benefits as education, jobs, and tenure, covert discrimination persuades them of their own inadequacy or deficiency.

That is what makes so many academic women think they are going crazy when covert discrimination first closes its grip on them. People seem to be lying to them even as they appear to offer good and friendly counsel. One thing doesn't square with another; this fact doesn't fit with that. I have met a number of women who endured experiences similar to mine. At first all of them thought that they had stumbled into the world of Kafka.

Covert discrimination cannot exist without falsehood. Occasionally the blame is laid to chance ("We just lost our tenure position"), but more often the blame is placed on the victim, who "was just not good enough."

You will cause the least trouble to the university if you can be persuaded to doubt your own worth and to believe that your opponents are being objective. The university may also rely on your fear of what will happen to you if you resist its authority. If, however, you do struggle, the university will put forth a powerful effort to get you to fight the case on its own grounds (usually the quality of your scholarship, occasionally the quality of your teaching). Those who have the power to practice discrimination understand its mechanisms far better than do their victims. Many of us are burdened with a sense of inferiority; though we know better, we are nevertheless likely to believe authorities who assure us in a seemingly rational and objective or even benevolent tone that our work is mediocre. People who possess the critical vocabulary, who know the lingo, can always find the words and means to support a predetermined negative judgment; all that is needed is the will to make that judgment. There are stock methods of creating such a negative assessment: discovering "inconsistencies" between parts of your work; distorting the argument; suggesting that the development lacks complexity; asserting that your work failed to include some other aspect of the subject.

When discrimination is being practiced, the publication of an article, even in a prestigious journal, is no longer a sufficient guarantee of the article's quality. At the upper levels of your consciousness you may know that your work is good, but the accumulation of years of social conditioning may have left you barely able, at the lower levels of your consciousness, to sustain your self-esteem. Those who practice covert academic discrimination seek to deprecate your achievements, to disparage your abilities, and to suggest that you have little promise of future growth. Covert discrimination is a form of psychic violence; it robs you of the merit of your accomplishments and levels a subtle but deadly assault on that quality you will most need, your belief in yourself. Under the hammer blows of "objectivity" or, worse, kindly authority, your self-esteem may disintegrate, and you may find yourself facing a severe or even incapacitating depression.

My department head told me that I was being denied tenure because of the mediocre quality of my publications; this was a department in which for years everyone else with a Ph.D. and some publications had received tenure. He admitted that I had been productive; the quality, not the quantity, of my publications was at issue. If my articles were that poor, I asked, how could I have succeeded in publishing them in reputable journals? All the other assistant professors I knew were struggling to get their work accepted for publication. My department head replied that an article isn't necessarily good simply because it gets published. Members of the dean's advisory council, which reviewed my case, asked the department chairman the same question and got the same answer; apparently, the department thought it could judge the quality of a person's work better than the journal editors could.

I reminded him that I had published as much as the last man who had received tenure and promotion; the chairman replied that they now thought that their decision to award tenure to the previous candidate had been a mistake.

I appealed up the line, from department to dean's office to president's office. Things got "curiouser and curiouser." My department head had obtained two outside letters of evaluation from scholars at other universities; these two letters were critical of my work. The department had never solicited outside letters for a candidate before I came up for tenure and has not solicited any since then. My department head withheld the names of the authors of the letters from members of departmental committees and removed the signatures from the letters before sending them to the dean's office. (He later said that he had obtained the letters solely for his own guidance and had never intended to read them to the committees. He did not explain why, if that was true, he had previously guaranteed anonymity to the authors of the letters.)

Members of the dean's advisory council protested that they would not read anonymous letters and demanded to know the identity of the authors. One had been written by an old friend of my department head who was teaching at a nearby university and whose wife was teaching in my department on a one-year appointment and had been seeking a permanent job. The other outside letter, which evaluated the portion of my work that was feminist criticism, came from an expert in Renaissance and seventeenth-century poetry. I have published nothing about Renaissance or seventeenth-century poetry. This scholar had published no feminist criticism.

To solicit the first outside letter, my department head had written his friend a letter, dated 6 September, asking him to read a couple of my articles and offering the following explanation: "We have a particularly difficult tenure decision. Our committee has already made its appraisal, but we'd like someone outside the university to be in on this one. Anonymity will be religiously kept." The committee referred to, however, did not even convene until several weeks after that letter was written. It did not make its "appraisal" until mid-November, months after the letter was written. The committee that read my work, visited my classes, and interviewed me then voted 5-0 to recommend me for tenure. A second committee then met with the first one, and at that point the outside letters were revealed. The committees' joint vote was 5-4; I was told that there was a two-thirds rule and that I had failed by one vote.

The dean's advisory council, when it heard my appeal, brushed aside violations of academic practice and irregularities in the procedures of the university. The message to me remained the same: my scholarship was just not good enough.

I had been an active feminist at the university. I had helped to publish a report about the status of women there and had presented a copy to HEW representatives when they came to investigate the status of women and minorities at the university. I had been told that these activities would not be held against me. They were supposedly unrelated to the pronouncement some months later that I was a poor scholar.

Months of struggle and appeal, during which I was repeatedly told that my work was mediocre, left me depressed and unable to continue my research. Had I not continued to fight by filing a lawsuit after I was denied tenure, I might still be convinced, at some deep level, of my inadequacy. The lawsuit uncovered many things that were never meant to be seen in the light of day. The records made it plain to me that I was as good as or better than men who received tenure before and after me and that procedures were manipulated in order to support a predetermined negative recommendation.

Ask, ask for whom the standards are raised; are they raised for you?

To File or Not to File

Selene Harding-Curd Weise

I am asked this question more often than any other: "How have you handled the emotional stress of fighting a federal case?" I have seen much psychological trauma left in the wake of civil rights cases, and in my experience as both litigant and observer I have come to believe that the trauma is greater than it need be. Developing an awareness of the pitfalls is the first step in avoiding them.

When a woman in academia believes she is being discriminated against, her first question is likely to be either "Am I really all that bad?" or "What should I have done differently?" Women still find it difficult to recognize discrimination, particularly when it is directed at them. But if you, a woman scholar, believe you have been the victim of unlawful discrimination, you must first determine whether you were indeed a victim.

Talk to trusted friends to see if the standards applied to you were the same as those applied to men in analogous positions. The weakest point in the armor of most universities is the lack of standardized personnel procedures and uniform academic criteria. It is unwise to broadcast your hurt and outrage. Wanting to sit down and howl is understandable, but don't succumb to the temptation. Be judicious in your choice of confidantes; the fewer the better.

The next step is to ascertain if the discrimination was illegal. For you, a scholar, the law library should hold no terrors, and that is the place to begin. Most law librarians will be willing to help you find your way through the literature, and on the way you will discover some of the best prose in North America.

There are statutes passed by the legislature, regulations pro-mulgated by agencies charged with administering the statute law, and case law. In our system of justice, much law is developed through court precedents, and so when you begin to look for laws that might apply to you, start with the law reviews. You will find review articles listed in a computer printout. Read those that look interesting, and make notes of the case law they quote. You will find that each case is brought to court under one or more laws or regulations. Then read the actual statute law or regulation. This seems like a backwards way of doing research, but for the novice the law reviews are the best way of finding a way through the thickets of regulations, laws, and some very conflicting case law. A word on conflicts: Supreme Court decisions take precedence over all other courts in the country. Next down the line are the nine federal appeals courts, and within their jurisdictions the appeals courts hold precedence. Although circuit courts listen to one another, they are not bound by one another's decisions. A decision by the ninth circuit, for example, does not bind the fourth circuit. Decisions by federal district courts are binding only within the same district. This may explain the mystifying conflicts in decisions. At this point you might wonder if you should have a lawyer. The answer is no. Later, maybe, but for now, save your money.

By the time you have talked to friends and spent some time in the law library, you should be ready to decide whether or not you have really been the victim of unlawful discrimination and, if so, whether you can prove it. The first requirement of a good case is documentation. If you have not saved routine correspondence, salary details, memos, contracts, and the other ephemera one accumulates in the course of professional life, you may be in for a rough time proving that anything untoward has been done to you. You may know that a certain document exists, but if the university can't find its copy, you are out of luck. Even when you have adequate documentation, you may have to persuade a judge or hearing examiner to accept the authenticity of your copy.

Let us assume that you have kept everything. What next?

This is the hard part. In your reading of case law, did you happen to notice how old some of those cases are? My own case is eleven years old, and there are others that are even older. The most important aspect of the decision as to whether or not to file a complaint is this: can you afford it over the long haul? Unless you have a job that is secure or have someone else to put bread on the table and keep a roof over your head, a civil rights case is not for you. Under no circumstances should you say, "If I win my case, I will get my job back and things will go on as before." Never depend on winning a case for your financial support. If you are fortunate enough to have a secure job or to have someone else with a secure job who is willing to grubstake this operation, then what? Well, how tough are you?

Fighting a civil rights case requires real toughness—not nastiness, but simply the ability to endure the harassment, the retaliation, and the lies. You will lose some friends, but you will find new ones in surprising places, and good old friends will be more loyal and loving than ever before. If you have a loving husband who is cool to the idea of your fighting a civil rights case, think long before taking it on. Every bit as important as financial backing is emotional support. Give yourself time to make this important decision. A civil rights case will effect profound changes in your life. In my own case, I am not unhappy with the changes—I like them.

Suppose that you have a good case, that you can prove it, and that a loving someone supports you and thinks it is great for you to fight for your rights. Suppose that you also have a cluster of friends who think the same thing and are prepared to support you. (Don't let your friends talk you into fighting, however. This is your case and you will pay the final price for it.) Are you sure that this is what you want to do with the next two or three (or many more) years of your life? Look up some of the women you have read about in the law books. Most of us are happy to discuss the emotional costs and rewards as well as the professional and personal disruptions involved in our cases.

Suppose that you have decided to fight. There are many stages, however, at which you can change your mind and drop the case without doing damage to yourself or to those who will come after you. Now that you have made your decision, what do you do next? In the telephone book under the government listings for your city or county, look for a division of human rights or an equal employment opportunity office or some other human rights agency. If there is none, look in the state listings. Most states now have a division of human rights, and the federal laws require that the Equal Employment Opportunity Commission defer to state agencies for sixty days after a case is filed. While you are making up your mind whether or not to file a complaint, remember that the statutes of limitations on civil rights cases are sometimes very short, and so don't be too slow to decide, or the calendar may make up your mind for you. Also, it is important to familiarize yourself with all regulations and time limits on filing and to learn what you must do and when. Remember that no one will ever be as concerned about these things as you will. Right from the beginning, you must get used to managing your own case.

When you have located the appropriate agency, state or local, make an appointment to file a complaint. Someone at the agency will probably write the complaint for you to make sure that the legal terminology is correct, but you are responsible for the facts. Don't politely sign something just because someone at the agency wrote it. People in government often do not understand the intricacies of academia, and it is easy to find yourself stuck with a passage in your complaint that is not quite accurate because you thought that passage concerned an insignificant detail. Also, it is better to put in too much information than to risk leaving out one important detail.

Stick to the facts, however, and leave the conclusions to the hearing examiner.

Now you have filed a complaint and walked out feeling unstrung, wondering what on earth you have done. What happens next? For what may seem an intolerably long time, probably nothing will happen. Just give it time. If you have filed a complaint against an employer for whom you are still working or if you are still a student (as I was), expect some retaliation. The degree and intensity of the reprisal may indicate how seriously your case is being taken. The size of the school and the amount of publicity your case receives will also be factors in the manner in which the university receives your complaint. If you complain against a major university with a long history of civil rights litigation, one more case will hardly cause a ripple. But if you are still working or are a student in the department against which you are complaining, the heat can become intense. Take all potentially useful documents home, copy them, and put the copies in a safe place. Otherwise they have a way of disappearing. People will do things under legal stress that they would not normally do. Don't leave things with a secretary on whom unbearable pressures can be applied. Some of your erstwhile colleagues are now your enemies. Take care.

Various groups on campus may want to espouse your cause. You are going to have to decide whether you want to fight your case on legal or political grounds. The two don't mix. If you have a case that you believe to be legally strong, stick to the law. Try to discourage publicity campaigns, demonstrations, picketing, and all the other devices, no matter how well they may work in other forums. Judges and hearing examiners resent any hint of external pressure. Political activity can benefit a case in only one way: If you can bring enough unfavorable public opinion to bear on the university, you might force a settlement. But don't count on it. Political actions work better in a small school in a small community where public pressure is more effective. Most universities have established policies for handling civil rights complaints; don't expect your school to deviate from those policies. They might change if a new administration comes to power or if the university loses a case. Who knows? The case it loses could be yours. And so, keep your head down, don't go public, and try to keep others from going public in your behalf, because that could generate retaliation against you, without doing your case any good. Also, guard against letting groups use your case for their own purposes. For example, you may be a member of a lesbian group, but unless you were terminated for being a lesbian, keep the subject out of your case. Stick to the professional reasons for which you were terminated. You may know privately that you were let go because you were too liberal, too conservative, too young, or too old, but unless a representative of the university used one of those labels to describe you, don't bring the issue up; it will muddy the water.

If you decide to hire a lawyer, don't look for a general attorney; civil rights law is a complicated specialty. If a general lawyer agrees to take your case, he or she might not know enough about civil rights law to win it. You need the best civil rights lawyer you can find, and such attorneys come in all shapes, colors, sexes, and sizes. You may find someone just out of law school, or you might try the civil rights organizations. If they cannot help you, they can usually give you the name of someone who can. Be prepared for a long, slogging search. Civil rights law doesn't pay very well, because few civil rights plaintiffs have enough money to pay for legal help, but try not to get discouraged. Keep your case moving while you look, and don't let time limits run out on you. If you have to file a paper to meet a deadline, talk to the law clerk and then file it yourself. Law clerks don't much like the plaintiff who goes *pro se* (for oneself), but if pushed a little they can be surprisingly helpful. Judges like *pro se* plaintiffs even less, but if you are faced with either dropping your case (which by this time you are convinced is a strong one) or going it alone, then go it alone. You have nothing to lose.

Look for a successful civil rights lawyer, preferably one who has won cases in court. Be wary, however, of the political lawyer. You want the facts of the case, not your lawyer, to be the issue when you get to court. Some of the best civil rights lawyers are probably people you have never heard of, but they will know the intricacies of civil procedure in federal court, and they will know how to get things done.

Another word of caution on the subject of lawyers. You may very well have several lawyers during the course of the litigation if your case goes to federal court. Remember that civil rights law does not pay well, and most lawyers cannot afford to see a case through from beginning to end. Don't be upset, and don't feel abandoned. Just ask your lawyer to help you find someone else before he or she moves on.

At some point, you must decide how far you will take the case. You cannot make that decision in advance, because sometimes outside factors affect the situation. In my own case, new laws passed by Congress made it possible to go further than I had anticipated. If you decide to file with the state division of human rights, it does not mean you have to fight all the way to the Supreme Court. At each stage of the case, you will reevaluate your chances of success at the next stage. At each step, whether you win or the university wins, the loser will probably appeal. Even if you win in the state division, you can depend on getting nothing, because the university will appeal. But if you lose, of course, you can appeal.

If no one wins, what is to be gained by fighting at all? Some plaintiffs do win, and they get either a job or a financial settlement, but more important, you can gain much from the fight itself. In my own case, I have won nothing concrete, but I am not finished yet. The Second Circuit Court of Appeals, however, handed down a good decision, which is being built on by other university women, and so my litigation has resulted in some good case law that will help others who come after me. But you must make the ultimate decision only after you have assessed your alternatives. For me the alternative of not fighting was unacceptable, and so I have gone through one forum after another with unexpected results: I have found a new profession, and I have grown as a person. I like myself better than I would have if I had knuckled under and accepted what the university did to me.

You must still face the problem of handling the emotional trauma of fighting a civil rights case, however. With all the preparation in the world, it will be a harrowing experience. (In my own case, I was hired as a lecturer in the department where I was also a graduate student. The appointment was turned down by the dean of the school and the position offered to an academically less qualified man.) I have since completed the Ph.D. To protect myself from academic retaliation, I rarely mentioned that I had filed a complaint against the university. After the initial flurry of publicity, most people, if they ever knew about the case, quickly forgot it. This meant that my academic life was as free of discrimination as it would have been if I had never filed. Also, I was politically active as a graduate student, and my activist colleagues were my staunchest friends and supporters. But the case was never the center of my life; working toward my degree was. Because I maintained a purely professional relationship with all except those actually named in the complaint, I had gained substantial support among faculty and administrators as well as among students by the time my case went to public hearing. If you cannot maintain your academic life, find another job—any other job— or continue your research on your own, but do something that will demand your attention and energy. Don't let the case take over your entire life. Obsessive interest in litigation can embitter the closest relationships, and, more important, it can embitter you. Try to channel your energy into some productive work, even if it isn't what you most want to do.

Accept what comes, and turn your fight to good account. You will learn new skills and new ways of looking at things. If you can develop an attitude of acceptance, you will be free to make the most of fighting the case, not just winning it. Do your best to win. Fight hard, and then accept what comes. The chances are it will be something good, win or lose.

Paying Your Dues, Part-Time

Joanne Spencer Kantrowitz

The only person I really envy is a dermatologist in Ravenna, Ohio. She's got it both ways: her profession, her colleague-husband, her children, and a high-paying part-time job with a posh office, a secretary, and absolute control over her time and income. She's the reason I advise women students to become independent doctors, lawyers, dentists, accountants and to avoid like the plague any work that involves the modern corporation. The university is such a corporation, a corporation that has failed the women Ph.D.'s it has so gratuitously educated. The Alma Mater is a woman of ill repute. At least she is so for the women of my generation who were educated in the 1950s and early 1960s. That perception is the reason I became an English department "troublemaker" in 1974.

There were two of us: Dr. Shirley Graham, a botanist, and I, both experienced teachers and published scholars. We found ourselves in the classic married woman–academic bind, handed part-time, leftover work and barred from standard appointments by practices and attitudes that failed to take into account our existence, our potential, or our accomplishments. Our complaints remain unresolved, despite two sessions in federal court and complaints to three government agencies. At the moment, our case is still in the hands of federal agencies. We have had the support of a U.S. representative from our state and the state chapter of the National Organization of Women, and the MLA. The next year should tell whether we have wasted our time in a futile assault on the institution or whether we are harbingers of real change. Only our male colleagues who fight us, either with direct action or with their indifference, can determine the outcome, for they hold the power over all of us. Only by taking such risks in many institutions can we women hope to change the work practices that stifle us or turn us into the "masculine woman" our adversaries so scorn.

Because our credentials were superior, Shirley and I deliberately decided to challenge the institution, but the men running the institution chose not to hear—for a variety of reasons, some rational, some emotional. This antagonism is hidden behind a variety of "principles." (Academics always find some principle to justify their actions; that is why academic politics are so arcane.) This essay will focus on my own view of our joint experience. Differences exist in the details of Shirley's complaint and of mine, but both complaints derived from the same external social facts: we were both married to academics employed at the same university as full professors; she had three small children, I had two. We had both chosen research and publication as major interests and we both felt that we belonged at a university. We both discovered, however, that the university had no use for us, except as casual, low-status laborers. All our lives, we had been forced to compromise our career interests to keep our families intact. Our husbands hated this compromise, but we were all caught in a world that brooked little deviation from that pattern. Thus, in 1974 when the chance for change came, we took it, and we became two families against the university. "Mama's court case" was a familiar phrase in our families and a reality we lived with at home, at school, in town. Our husbands functioned as supporters and advisers at home, but Shirley and I had to do battle. And we did.

THE BACKGROUND

From studies of women Ph.D.'s, we know that only about half of them are married, in contrast to most male professors, who, of course, reflect the general population profile in which bachelors are a small minority. Women, in general, are concentrated in colleges and junior colleges and are underrepresented on the university level, where greater opportunities for research and professional status exist. Fifty-five percent of the women in the MLA are married, and thirty-eight percent have dependent children. This suggests that at least half of the women in our profession live in dual-career households. (See MLA Commission on the Status of Women, "Study III," *PMLA*, 91, 1976, 124–36, esp. p. 131; and John Centra, *Women, Men and the Doctorate*, Princeton: Educational Testing Service, 1974, esp. pp. 159–60.)

I was one of those who married and began working toward a Ph.D. at the same time, before the palmy days of subsidized graduate study began in the mid 1960s. It took me nine years (1958–67) to finish at the University of Chicago. Course work and examinations from 1958 to 1963 were followed by four years in New York during which I produced two articles, a 150-page dialect study, and finally a dissertation that required additional work in areas unrelated to my graduate courses. I entered the academic labor market in 1964 and since then have taught at five different institutions. Except for one job, from 1967 to 1969, all my work was on temporary appointment at the undergraduate level. For two of those years I even commuted a hundred miles a day. I have taught at three eastern women's colleges, one technical institute, and one state university.

I did all this happily, did not count the cost or the time, because I had wholeheartedly imbibed the ethic of excellence, merit, and hard work that my male professors so eloquently preached during my student days. By 1977 I had become the possessor of a vita listing three books in three different areas and a clutch of articles, long and short. I was professionally active, too, and emerged on the national level as an originator of a teaching newspaper in medieval-renaissance studies. In 1974 I found myself quoted in the *Chronicle of Higher Education, Newsweek,* and the Sunday *New York Times.* In 1977 I even became an expert reader for *PMLA.* By then, some kind men were even saying that my scholarly work was remarkable. Obviously, I had arrived.

Wrong. What I was was a faculty wife who had had the temerity to complain about the terms of her part-time status and who was the object of an infuriated chairman's "meat ax" (the phrase is his). I had indeed arrived—at the brutish realities of life for an academic woman who does not follow the male work pattern and who dares to marry and have children.

Looking back at my student days, I remember twelve women in a group of thirty-seven Ph.D. candidates during the years from 1958 to 1963. Of those twelve, seven finished the Ph.D., but only three hold regular appointments. Of those three, only one married and had children. The rest of us have worked, at intervals and in odd corners, while we had our babies and did our research. I am the only one who received a postdoctoral research award: $1,000 from ACLS in 1971. Seven out of the twelve continue "in the profession," but only three are regular faculty. Why?

Still, the professors say, in genuine wonderment, "Why don't the women do more?" An answer: because the modern American university imitates the corporate structure our nation so cherishes and that structure recognizes only conventional (i.e., male) categories. The university takes in its favored few and processes them through the stages of the academic hierarchy. Exceptions are made, but those exceptions rarely reflect the special conditions of women's lives. The system can allow for any number of variations, such as military service, research leave, "community service," alcoholism, divorce, sexual promiscuity, serious physical or mental illness, but never marriage or motherhood: no maternity leave, no schedules adjusted to child-rearing needs, and so on. The "solution" for such "female trouble" is part-time, temporary status.

The origins of the part-time teacher are cloudy. A few are employed at liberal arts colleges where teaching is the primary focus of the institution and where a student-faculty ratio of ten-to-one or fifteen-to-one is jealously guarded. Some elite universities maintain a comparable stance and ratio. Public universities, by and large, have used part-time and teaching fellows as cheap labor to accommodate the enormous number of undergraduates they attempt to educate. In the late 1960s and 1970s junior colleges followed suit. With the oversupply of Ph.D.'s and the economic depression, part-time labor has recently become an attractive means of cost cutting in the "labor-intensive industry" of higher education. That is, classes can be covered by a part-timer for approximately half the wages of a full-time professor, without the cost of fringe benefits and with no commitment to tenure or permanent employment.

Before 1972 my experience with part-time work was very limited. I had done just enough to see what a bad deal it was: last-minute course assignment, generally to freshman composition (with all the sections one could wish), or a chance to teach an introductory literature course, which was regarded as a privilege. I always received a flat fee. In New York, in 1964, the pay was $750 per semester course. By teaching six such semester courses a year, I could earn $4,500, but I had little time for anything else if I did a good job. By tacit agreement, anyone teaching such a load cut as many corners as possible, usually in the interest of finishing a dissertation and getting a "real" job. The interview for such a job almost had a scenario. The chairman played the academic wise man while I, the applicant, played the earnest young scholar. In every instance, there came a moment when the man mentioned the salary—always negligible—and then sweetened it with some sort of murmur about colleagueship. That was my cue to reassure him and demonstrate that I was not a crass materialist but an idealistic young professional. So the deal was made, with pretense all around. I pretended in the hope of something better; he pretended in order to avoid looking at the reality of his hiring practice: cheap labor, no status.

After one such experience in 1964, I did not work part-time again until 1972. In 1969 I agreed to move to a state university where my husband wished to accept a new job. That was when I made my major career mistake, giving up a regular spot at a Catholic women's college, but our search for two jobs had been futile, our first son was born in 1968, my husband unexpectedly won a Ford Fellowship that took us to Oxford, and we hoped to have a second child. In June 1970 we returned from England to find ourselves at a newly expanded state university that was floundering in disarray and panic after a major student protest.

During the expansive 1960s I had had a hard time finding work in the New York area. I remember sending out about thirty letters, which resulted in two or three interviews during which I was questioned about my husband and his career plans. My favorite rejection letter was one in 1967 regretting the university's choice of another candidate but asking me if I would take a part-time position. Answering that my interest would depend on the money and the courses, I received neither a response nor an offer. In 1965 two colleges of the City University were similarly uninterested, but a private women's college picked me up as a temporary lecturer for two years. At the time, I assumed all this reflected the particularly competitive work world of New York. Later, in my native Midwest, I learned that such attitudes and practices are typical of my profession.

My second child was born in September 1971, and I deliberately sought a part-time job the following year. My reasons were personal: the move had been difficult; the birth not easy; the family plagued with illness. It had been a hard year. Beyond that, I was stuck on the publishing issue. While in England, I had substantially revised my dissertation, but I could not find a publisher. (We were later to learn that book publication in the humanities had fallen off by thirty percent during the early 1970s.) I then began to turn the dissertation into articles, only to learn how long the consideration process can take. In the spring of 1972, five years beyond the Ph.D., I had one article and one review in print and seven items in finished form under consideration, all the way from books to one-page notes. In five years, I had also moved twice—once to England, once into our first house—borne two sons (with a miscarriage in between) over a four-year span, taught full-time for two years, built a base in Neo-Latin drama and rhetoric at Oxford for further work on the morality play. I knew that if I were to emerge as a scholar I could not manage a full-time teaching load, two sons—one three and a half years old and the other six months old—and continue research. I chose to teach part-time in order to conserve my mental energy and to see if scholarly publication were indeed my future. At the time, I thought a Ph.D. from an elite university counted for something. I was soon to be disabused of that illusion.

So I played the part-time interview game again. At one university, the chairman waved me on, after a routine question or two about research. The young man in charge of freshman English enjoyed an academic gossip with me (we had had the same teachers at the university where he had done his Ph.D.; I, my B.A.) and apparently assumed I was available, for, without my consent, he later sent me a schedule of courses and a list of texts. The salary: $750 per quarter

course. At the university where my husband taught, the procedure
was much more elaborate. I was taken to lunch by the chairman, then
interviewed by the man in charge of undergraduate studies. I was
asked if I was interested in graduate teaching: they were a bit short in
the seventeenth century. I was so flattered that I responded with a
long letter detailing my interest in research and graduate teaching. I
was told I was being hired for a year to replace a linguist who was
on leave but that there was some possibility of future, regular
appointment. No, he couldn't appoint me as an adjunct or visiting
associate professor because it would create morale problems in the
department. He explained:

> The problem is that in your case the total amount of actual
> teaching experience adds up to something a little over five years
> despite the fact that you have been engaged in one way or
> another in the profession for some time. If there were several
> more articles like the one in *PQ*, it would be a different matter.
> But unfortunately the department these days is in a mood to
> make the Associate Professorship reasonably hard to get—
> partly perhaps in reaction to its having been too easy to get in
> the past.
>
> I should like to make clear that I'm not putting down your
> credentials, which are a little different than those of someone
> who has been engaged full-time in the profession since leaving
> school.
>
> Were it possible to continue your appointment on an extended
> basis rather than for the one year only—and right at this point I
> have no idea where it will be possible—you wouldn't be
> considered as joining us with a fresh appointment at the
> Assistant Professor level. Your time in grade at other colleges
> would certainly be considered. I can never really anticipate what
> the Promotions Committee will decide, but, were you to join us
> on a permanent basis, especially on a full time appointment, I
> feel sure that early promotion (or an appointment as an
> Associate Professor) could come along soon.

Then followed an elaborate plan whereby I would be paid on a
prorated basis at a full salary of $12,000. The full-time course load, I
was told, was nine courses per year, or three per quarter. When I
questioned this, with the information that sociology (my husband's
department) had a course load of six courses per year, the chairman
smilingly assured me that the English department did things
differently. Four years later, I found that five people in a department
of fifty taught nine courses during 1972–73. The rest taught from four
to eight, depending on their publication record.

What really happened that year was that I taught five courses over three quarters for $6,667; they were Shakespeare, Survey of Middle English Literature, Sophomore Survey (Beowulf to Milton), and two sections of the History of the English Language. In 1972–73, although I had a Ph.D. and some publication, my pay was basically $1,333 per course. But the rhetoric sweetened the deal this time, and the chairman made expansive speeches on women's liberation. Sometimes he called me a linguist; sometimes he called me a medievalist; but he introduced me at the first department meeting as "Mrs. Kantrowitz, a faculty wife who taught at Vassar." I should have been warned by that, for "a faculty wife who taught at Vassar" was what I became in 1972, the year the university published its affirmative action program. Yes, the rhetoric was liberal, but nothing had changed at all.

THE COMPLAINT

Everything happened at once during my first year in my new job. Two of my long articles, one short one, and two notes appeared in print with very brief intervals between acceptance and publication. In July the University of Nebraska Press accepted my book for publication under a Mellon grant. An idea for a teaching publication in medieval-renaissance studies was scheduled for presentation at a committee meeting of the Mediaeval Academy in November 1973. All this happened in the first six months of 1973. I had been told that I would be retained at the same salary for another year, but with my teaching load reduced to four courses. But all talk of a full-time appointment was in abeyance. In July I had still not received a contract when I read in the local paper that the department had appointed a new man at the same title I held, visiting assistant professor. Book contract in hand, I sought the chairman and was told, "You and the other part-time women are now on quarter contracts." That was the beginning of my complaint.

It was to be three years before I finally knew what had happened, and the information came only as a result of the lawsuit. I had petitioned the department in December 1973 after four months of trying to work it out informally. That petition went unanswered, but the chairman kept telling me about his plans for creating permanent part-time positions, using me as his arguing point, for I had a "good degree" and "good credentials." Nothing tangible occurred, however, and the contracts continued to arrive at the end of each term when the teaching was almost over. In the spring of 1974 I was told I had to exhaust the university appeal process before I could file a government complaint. I did so, with supporting letters from the affirmative action officer and the faculty ombudsman. The provost simply referred the matter back to the department and told me, in effect, that government complaints took forever—that is, he was not concerned about affirmative action complaints, for the university was in good shape on that ground.

At the same time, I watched the fortunes of the new visiting assistant professor. His father, the chairman of the English department at a prestigious university, was the friend of a distinguished professor in our department. His record was sterling, a model of the late 1960s Ph.D. from Harvard. His dissertation was on the Reformation lyric from 1570 to 1620; mine was on a Reformation play dated 1552. He was told that a full-time load was seven courses and that the department wished him to publish in seventeenth-century literature, although he could, of course, publish in other areas as well. He was assigned to graduate courses in that area, and his schedule was filled out with the undergraduate courses I was eligible to teach: Shakespeare, drama, Senior Survey (Beowulf to Milton). In his second year, he was given a quarter off for research. His initial hiring overlapped the advertising required by law. The following year, the department powers made his appointment regular with the first year (officially temporary) counted toward tenure. His second appointment was not advertised, nor did most people know the details of it until the letters appeared as evidence in our complaint.

This procedure was standard department practice. It changed only in 1976. Recruiting activities were never general knowledge; there was no public departmental introduction of candidates. The chairman appointed the hiring committee, and the rank and file often found out about a new person only when he or she appeared in the fall. In my own case, the hiring had been done completely informally, and the chairman had not even bothered to send for my dossier. Outside evaluations were not routine for promotion and tenure either; the chairman said, "People just ask their friends, anyhow."

Looking back, I can see that the department had never included a woman who published much, let alone a book or two. As a modernist department, it focused on lyric poetry, the novel, and American literature. The senior professors from the earlier periods had lost a bitter battle that split the department in 1970. My research interests were in narrative allegory and pre-Shakespearean drama, areas outside the interests of the chairman and his friends. They wanted a faculty wife to teach their required linguistics, another area in which they had little interest. If I knew what was good for me, I'd stay in my place or, as I was told by my seniors, the chairman would see that I got "the meat ax," he'd tie me up in red tape in the process, and I would get no credit for previous experience. That was true; there was no way I could survive within the university structure. If I didn't like it, I could get a job somewhere else—maybe in one of the "little ladies' colleges" I'd come from.

Except for some murmurs, my colleagues stayed clear of the situation. So I filed my complaint and moved into the government arena where the rules for fighting gave me a chance. At that point, members of the department investigated my credentials. Thereafter, they did not question my achievements; the argument now became one of specialization. They had never hired anyone in my area, they said. The man who was a visiting assistant professor was a seventeenth-century specialist; I was not. I was a linguist, a medievalist, a generalist, an undergraduate teacher—everything but what their specifications called for. Of course, they did the specifying. The same tactic was used against my co-complainant, whom I met for the first time in the spring of 1974. We would both be "let go," not fired, for the university had no contractual obligations to us, or so its spokesmen said. Of course, they'd throw a little work our way, if we behaved ourselves and apologized. Just sign, and you can be a part-time academic once more. I had violated the unspoken sexual rules of the university, and I was under no illusion that utopia lay somewhere else. So we took our stand, reluctantly but firmly. Dr. Shirley Graham, the scientist, and I, the humanist, joined forces.

Shirley holds a Ph.D. in botany (Michigan, 1963). She is a former Fulbright scholar (Copenhagen) with a postdoctoral year at Harvard, the author of some twenty-five articles, and a member of two national professional committees. She sometimes collaborates with her husband, whose specialty (paleobotany) is different from hers (systematics). She started teaching at the university in 1964 during the days of the nepotism rule; her three children were born in 1967, 1969, and 1971. The department let her use her husband's lab and an office; she regularly taught only the introductory labs and was available on short notice to "fill in." Her salary was never more than $3,500. By 1974, after ten years, her title was part-time temporary associate professor.

In September 1974 Shirley and I retained a lawyer and filed formal complaints with the state office of civil rights, the EEOC, and HEW. Of the three, only the one at HEW came to fruition, and that did not occur until December 1976, in the middle of our private legal suit. In the meantime, the English department remained unchanged. In November 1974, congruent with my government complaints, the department considered me for promotion. No one explained how the department could promote someone on a quarter-by-quarter contract or what the promotion was good for. I cooperated, skeptically. The committee vote was nine to eight in my favor (missing the two-thirds requirement). This time, the basis for the chairman's refusal to recommend me was the argument that I had not served enough time in rank; that argument, of course, contradicted his initial evaluation and failed to take my previous experience into account. From then on, I simply filed the usual appeals, which were always returned with a quotation from the policy book to the effect that part-time appointments held no faculty rights. Finally, in 1976, the new provost ordered a part-time procedure that limited hiring to two of three quarters, or twenty weeks, in effect avoiding federal legislation on work benefits. I had worked four years under these terms, had published one book (with two more forthcoming), had established a reputation on the national level, was being asked to referee manuscripts, and was a litigant against the university. My colleagues now offered me a position in a part-time pool at a salary of $875 per course. Of course, I quit. I had never been hired in the first place. I was only a faculty wife.

This, then, was the history of my experience during the time the university and my male colleagues were proclaiming their adherence to the principle of affirmative action. Hired under false premises and liberal rhetoric, I was introduced and treated as a faculty wife. When I dared to complain, I met outrage and retaliation and indifference from the higher administrators, and, later, from the new faculty union. In 1976 Graham and Kantrowitz filed suit in federal court under Title VII. Now the university's lawyers entered, and our lawyer was no match for them.

When we hired our lawyer, few attorneys were willing or able to take on women's lawsuits. The Women's Law Fund was not interested; it was busy with working-class women; an eminent labor lawyer in the area refused to take us seriously; the head of the local NOW chapter suggested a young man, recently out of law school who was willing to take the case on a contingency basis, the only way we could afford a lawyer over a period of time. At the time, neither he nor we had any idea how long and involved the fight would be. He had successfully negotiated such complaints with area businesses and was building a career in public-interest law. We checked on him with a sociologist friend who was active in local politics. All reports were good, and he stayed with us for almost three years, but collapsed in the end.

The first suit, filed under Title VII, came to trial within six months after we filed it. The judge, a male, was both respected and feared for his strict court procedure. He ran the case with an iron hand while the university's lawyer used every possible tactic to delay. Finally, on the third appearance, when trial seemed inevitable, the university's attorney asserted that he was empowered to represent only the individuals, not the university. At that point, our lawyer advised us to dismiss the suit and refile. This process took about two months, at which point the university lawyer successfully argued that the "right to sue" granted by EEOC was invalid, because its time limit had passed. Cut off from Title VII, the case was then entered under Section 1984, that is, the more general Fourteenth Amendment. That suit was set for trial on 8 March 1977.

In the meantime, in September 1976, HEW reappeared; the investigation was completed in ten weeks, and findings of discrimination were issued on 1 December. During those three months, we were in constant touch with the investigators and supplied them with copies of official documents that were not among the university's submissions. The head of the faculty union then put us in touch with the AAUP lawyer, although he seemed to share the dean's opinion that the university would negate the HEW findings on appeal. In January we were the subject of almost daily newspaper stories in the three area newspapers. At this point, the leader of the one campus women's group offered her support, and we mounted a political pressure campaign on the campus, complete with resolutions to the board of trustees.

Concurrently, our lawyer accepted a job in Washington and closed his local practice in the fall of 1976. We had little contact with him until February. He did not follow up our contacts with AAUP in December or, later, with a local chapter of the American Civil Liberties Union. The day before the pretrial hearing, our lawyer flew in for a session with the HEW representatives and the university's lawyers. The head of the regional federal civil rights office, accompanied by the HEW lawyer, also arrived, having spent three days going over our case. They came equipped with their own legal research. Our lawyer was late and not particularly interested. We took them all to the session with the university lawyers. That session seemed pointless. Our adversaries indeed asked us what we'd settle for, but most of the session seemed designed to intimidate us with descriptions of appeals and countersuits they could wage against us. They wanted us to settle for $10,000 each. We were interested in regular jobs and in changing university policy. We were flexible on the subject of back wages, although HEW later came up with a figure of $51,000 for me; $66,000 for Shirley Graham. But we had already told our lawyer that such a flat settlement was not acceptable.

The next day at the pretrial hearing, the judge set up the rules for the trial. He refused delaying motions from the university, called for a compression of their witness list, accepted ours but reserved the right to rule on the inclusion of our witnesses on the affirmative action policy. The issue seemed to turn on the question of whether the university had followed procedure or had been arbitrary, terms we all know are the cutting edge. He attempted, but failed, to settle the suit in chambers. Finally, as we were all leaving, he called back the lawyers and ordered the university to offer $11,000 to each of us. After a long interval, the offer came through as notes in our lawyer's hand. Exhausted, Shirley wished to end it there, but I objected to the riders attached. In a dramatic scene in the hallway, our lawyer dashed back into the hearing room, with me shouting behind him, and emerged ten minutes later to run off to a divorce case in another court. Then followed twenty-four hours of conferring with the HEW group and, finally, a Sunday appointment with our lawyer. He presented us with legal documents to sign. We were to (1) drop all government complaints by signing the letters written for us; (2) never apply for employment at the university again; (3) issue no public statements whatsoever. For all this, we would each be paid $11,000, with one third as the lawyer's fee. The case was settled, and he would under no conditions do anything more. I left in a cold rage, not knowing what I would do, but knowing that I would not drop the complaints and I would not keep quiet. I saw that the university was trying to quash two actions for the price of one and to immobilize HEW at the same time. And I saw that our lawyer had failed us, for he finally told us on Sunday that the $10,000 figure came from his consultation with two of his law professors and the judge's law clerk. We knew none of this beforehand, but it also explained why he had failed to make contact with the AAUP or ACLU. It seemed that the case had grown too big for him. He was out of the local area and out of touch with the developments of the last six months, he was burdened with financial losses, and he wanted out—preferably with pay.

We then pulled a counterattack: we made copies of the documents of agreement and released them to the newspapers. The headlines read, "Women Refuse Keep-Quiet Deal." Having thrown all our eggs in the HEW basket, we reinstated the EEOC complaint and sat back to wait. We thus became clients of the U.S. government, waiting for the wheels of the gods to grind once more. We had made a few points, after a year in court, but we had not won yet.

"AFFIRMATIVE" ACTION?

At this point in the narrative, most people would probably say, "Why bother?" Some of my male friends have said as much. My reply is a simple and an old one. In every life, there are moments when one chooses to stand. We nominate ourselves for these chores, and our motives are an amalgam of self-interest and social duty. Choosing to do so, we choose pain and turmoil, but we also choose the excitement that every politician knows: that our action may have positive results. It is an act of faith, a risk, because every politician also knows that, once unloosed, the outcome of such an action depends on things beyond anyone's control: public opinion and support, timing, the personalities involved, the twists and turns of unpredictable events, the threat and shame of losing.

Two perceptions were central in my decision to fight the university. One was an awareness of the position of women in academia, a position that was confirmed by my own experience. The other was a sense of outrage at the corporate structure of the university, a reformer's sense of disgust at an institution gone decadent.

At the university, from 1973 to 1977, I watched an organization break down. The breakdown could be attributed partly to the unrest of 1970. Too, there was the economic problem. Each year the rumors of faculty cuts would circulate or the president would announce their imminence, and each year they did not materialize. Enrollment dropped by ten percent in 1973–74, and it never recovered, but the student–faculty ratio stayed around twenty-six-to-one. The only real changes were low raises and few replacements when faculty left or retired. Each department adapted as best it could.

The turmoil was primarily psychic, I believe. The university had doubled in size during the 1960s, and half its faculty were hired after 1965. The older faculty were, by and large, local, politically conservative, and teaching-oriented. The new faculty were ambitious of reputation: their official idol was research "productivity." Within this old-new tension, the usual rhetoric of merit and excellence rang out, but it was applied erratically, as it usually is. A new president was hired in 1972. He was selected primarily by a group of influential new faculty who mobilized the faculty senate and the student government against the local candidate. The new president proved a questionable choice. During his five-year term, a good deal of administrative turnover occurred, and during our three-year complaint period, we dealt with two deans, two provosts, and three affirmative action officers. Administrative confusion was rampant.

During the same period, the university fought a suit against the Labor Department, which was acting on behalf of the female custodial workers. (The male union head who had originally filed the suit was fired.) The finding of discrimination in our case against the College of Arts and Sciences was joined by a similar finding against the computer division. A young staff member left the university's affirmative action office for a better job and filed a complaint with EEOC; a colleague of mine, on early retirement from the English department, filed a complaint against the international study program. And a tenured male associate professor of education was fired, and he sued the university. Amid such chaos, any attempt to change the institution from within was doomed. By and large, the shifting administrators were playing strictly by the rule book. "Cover yourself" was a term one heard over and over again.

Over the years, we were to learn that the university had its own definition of affirmative action and its own means of selecting deserving women. We began, in relative innocence, assuming the university's good faith and our colleagues' support. Eventually, we were stripped of both illusions. What we were really working against was the attitudes of our male colleagues and a supporting cadre of faculty wives who were outraged at our impertinence.

The most ferocious attack came from the chairman of the English department, who had initially presented himself as a proponent of the women's movement. In him, I discovered the strange phenomenon of the colleague who equates all women faculty with his own wife. His wife was a musician with an M.A. who had taught part-time for twenty-odd years. He told me she was a professional; he was devoted to her and to their three children, all students at the university. He told me often about his wife, and I heard about other men's wives, too. The first dean's wife was an ABD in anthropology with tenure as an assistant professor. The first provost's wife had a B.A. in Portuguese and had taught part-time for a while. But wives with Ph.D.'s usually teach in the branch campuses, which are really junior colleges. They never transfer to the main campus, although they are officially members of the main department, which heavily influences hiring and promotion in the branches. There the teaching loads are heavier and restricted to general courses for the first two years. The women commute from the town, while the men work on the main campus and teach graduate courses.

Two part-time colleagues of mine epitomized the faculty-wife role. Both of them held M.A.'s. Their husbands were well-established English professors of long tenure. The chairman labeled all faculty in terms of their specialties; these two women, I learned, were specialists in children's literature. During that period, everyone who taught children's literature was female, an anomaly I rather wondered about. It was, of course, an education course as well and consequently low-status in the English department.

These two women later became the chairman's example for his program on part-time appointments, his answer to affirmative action. The proposed policy was shepherded through the faculty senate by the husband of one of them, a man who headed the committee on academic policy and standards. (The name of his wife, who holds an M.A., later appeared on the list of university witnesses that was presented during our court case.) In July 1976, after two years, the senate passed that policy. Then it lay dormant, without action from the president or the board of trustees. This new status was for "individuals who have special qualifications which enable them to help a unit meet a continuing programmatic need that is beyond the resources of the full time faculty," as defined by the department. Stripped of its legalese, the policy offered one-year contracts, regular faculty status and requirements (research, teaching, and service), but no tenure. It proposed yearly review and renewal, apparently ad infinitum, or until the special need disappeared and the job ended. By contrast, a professor shifting to part-time status would retain his tenure. In the summer of 1977 the university resurrected this document for HEW, which found it discriminatory.

The university's efforts at "affirmative action" in those years all had a strange twist. During 1975–76, the new dean appointed an associate dean. His choice, a woman in her late fifties, was the widow of a track coach. She had taken an M.A. at the university in 1960, had been a useful teacher and an assistant professor for ten years or so. She was the dean's next-door neighbor and a close friend of the former dean's wife. Everyone liked her. The dean promoted her to associate professor, too, despite her department's negative vote, which followed directives on publication requirements. Then there was the wife of the chairman of the language department. Also an M.A., she had won a Distinguished Teaching Award on the basis of student votes. Initially denied tenure at the college level, she was granted it on appeal, with the help of friends in the English department. The other Distinguished Teacher, however, a male with a Ph.D. in philosophy, was denied tenure because, he was told, he hadn't published. Moreover, the year before, in the language department itself, two women with M.A.'s had been denied tenure, although one of them had almost completed the Ph.D. And then there was the M.A. in math who was promoted by the president; her husband was a personable grantsman in math and a friend of a trustee. Yet two male ABDs in the language department were denied promotion for lack of the Ph.D., although one had published.

In Shirley Graham's department, four positions were filled with men while the fifth, on the dean's orders, went to a woman zoologist who had taught on temporary contracts for years and had published little. Some members of that department protested, but the dean ignored them. That department then contained two women Ph.D.'s, neither of whom was active in scientific publishing. The dean's letter ordering this "quota" appointment later became part of the HEW evidence, since such action clearly violated affirmative action principles: you appoint a woman not because she is a woman but because she is clearly qualified. But "qualifications" depend on the judgment of those men who control the committee and who frame the job requirements.

If one wonders why there is hostility among men toward affirmative action, these kinds of confusions account for it. Besides, such promotions do the women's movement no good, for less qualified women cannot gain the authority or academic stature women need in the academic world. I began to understand why nepotism rules were instituted; the men in power appeared to be trading jobs for their wives with the M.A. as the "credential." Affirmative action was still a man's game with women kept in secondary roles.

While all this was happening, Shirley and I became the scandal. No one seemed to wonder why women with our qualifications should meet resistance while women without our qualifications were promoted. Even though we were teaching in the institution, we were passed over with the excuse that there were no openings in our specialties. Moreover, it became a matter of principle: government interference in the academy (the chemistry professor heading the faculty senate told us this government interference was just like what happened during the McCarthy era); the right of the senior faculty as specialists to control access and balance (in an excessively modernist department of English; in a biology department under pressure for evidence of publication). And all the sexist clichés started coming out from under the rug.

Shirley Graham went to a faculty wives' tea and arrived just in time to hear a colleague's wife say, "And she thinks she's worth $17,000. Why she's trying to take bread out of our children's mouths." I had met similar outrage. We were faculty wives just like them; we couldn't possibly be worth all that. Not what their husbands were worth.

CAUSES: THE LOCKER-ROOM MENTALITY

I began to see that the terms were genuinely sexual and that we were living through a period when sexual confusion was rife. I had lived my life assuming I was a remarkable woman. All my friends were, too. Perhaps we were reacting to the old image of the intellectual woman, but my group cultivated the feminine graces. Our houses were decorated with wit. It was a game with us; we could turn a hovel into a castle and we could do it on the cheap. We cooked like maniacs and our parties were adventures in who could think up what. We seldom wore pants suits because we always liked skirts better. We had our hair done, our toenails painted. We drank beer and wine, the bubblier the better. We laughed a lot, at ourselves and everyone else. And we earned our Ph.D.'s and wrote our articles in the same way that we lived—with wit and passion and brains. No wonder we had a tough time. We half thought everybody was like us; we were wrong. I began to understand why the early Christian virgins mutilated their faces with their own nails. We weren't even beautiful, but we were exceptional: we were women with Ph.D.'s, husbands, and beautiful small children. We had some more to learn.

During the 1960s attitudes toward sexuality began to change, but no one quite knew how. In the public mind, the women's movement was identified with braless flappers and promiscuous sex; so some men assumed that it was permissible to discuss one's sexual exploits with women present, extending the old male braggart game into mixed company. In the last ten years, everyone had been talking up a storm, but the new sex, far from liberating anybody, caused more trouble than it was worth. I'd been busy having babies, moving, and writing, so I was totally unprepared for the sexual anxiety that was running through that university and other places.

About this time tales circulated in our department, which had been shaken a few years earlier by the antics of a leading professor with a taste for graduate students. Stories abounded of other liaisons, between junior professors and the wives of senior colleagues, between faculty and students. Ten of the fifty faculty members in one department were said to be sexually involved with students; some later marrying, others not. Most members of the department greeted these stories with sympathy, in line with liberalism and the "new morality."

I didn't pay much attention to these matters until I started hearing from worried undergraduate women, some of whom went to faculty parties, nervous tales of sexual pressure. And then I, too, became the object of a certain kind of sexual hazing during a time when I was working night and day to meet my professional and family commitments. I began to wish for the old days when a strict line existed between students and faculty and when sex was a delicate subject, treated with discretion.

At the same time, the double standard still held. A young woman professor who had slept with perhaps the most sexually promiscuous member of the department received nothing but scorn for that misstep. She was bright and wrote decent articles, but few thought she would get tenure. The men said the faculty wives considered her a wicked woman. Fortunately, she found a better job before the test came.

I heard these tales in coffee room and hallway. And then, of course, there was the men's locker room. A noontime exercise group functioned as a major communications network, since it brought together, daily, men of all ages from the faculty, the administration, and the town. While they changed clothes and showered, they naturally talked—or gossiped, to use the "feminine" phrase. One of the advantages of husband-wife faculty was that I rapidly learned the useful information that my husband gained through that group, information I never heard except through him. Comparable exchange of opinion and fact occurred in the men's restrooms, where the men assembled after meetings. (A woman friend at another school told me she had noticed a decline in her information when her woman chairman was replaced by a man and she no longer heard the informal news in the restroom.)

Via the locker room, one could check university opinion. When the president appointed a woman vice-president for publicity, he chose from the athletics department. The men resented that choice, partly because so many academics are intolerant of "jocks," particularly in areas where football is a way of life. Their hostility took the form of sexual comment in the locker room, and the woman's sexual activity was detailed all the way back to high school. No one talked about her qualifications; the joke was she slept with the president: the age-old assumption by men who resent power in women.

But the locker room served another function, too. It became a conduit of information during our legal action, when my husband was regularly questioned about his wife's activities. For a year, one professor of English pumped him for useful information. My colleague never asked me, although he saw me often. When we spoke, his conversation was bland and conciliatory. Before the trial, he even tried—via the locker room—to get a copy of a manuscript my husband and I had written. Of course, at that point the professor's friends, my adversaries, were having an expert witness evaluate my scholarship, and the manuscript they wanted was the only major piece of my work that was then unpublished. My husband, of course, gave him only bland or confusing responses and told him to ask me. A regular evening feature in our household was our discussion of his current questions and the sort of answers we should give him next. This nonsense was typical of an atmosphere where trust and direct dealing no longer existed.

Then there were the other groups. A regular feature of the department was the weekly poker game. Of course, that group was made up of male professors only. The university also had a research group that met monthly to hear one another's papers. By invitation only and never held publicly, this group's meetings were also for men only.

These patterns are woven into the fabric of university life. Although less noticeably, they are also transmitted to professional associations whose meetings sometimes resemble business conventions, when men are away from home for a few days and feeling their oats. One begins to understand why some professional women develop a brusque tone in dealing with men. They prefer a reputation for "masculinity" to the problems of fending off unwanted sexual gestures. And they have learned that the males must identify the character of a woman's sexuality for diverse reasons: a few in hope of an easy liaison; others to reassure themselves that the woman is not interested. The games go on at the meetings, too, and they can overwhelm an unwary woman, for the men love to haze. There is always someone at a meeting to carry tales back home where tenure decisions are made: there, the men, uncomfortable with the new feminism, will disapprove of antics in a woman that they vicariously enjoy in some of their male friends. Sexual liberation is a myth. There is still the libertine, the prude, and the faithful lover, and our colleagues still judge a woman's sexuality by different standards, whether we like it or not. Feminist theories of self-assertion that omit this male fact ignore reality.

In the face of these institutions and attitudes, what can a professional woman do? Obviously, group political action is the only answer, and at some universities some groups are acting. At this university, the organization is poor because the campus women's group is new and is short on faculty leadership. It grew out of the AAUP Committee W, which had done a fine job producing reports on faculty salaries but the group was inexperienced and timid about campus politics. It helped my co-complainant and me enormously for two months in 1977 and acted as a pressure group within the university, but its resources scarcely went beyond that push. Besides, in strict political terms, women are a minority on any campus, in lower-paid positions, and cannot hope to win without the support of substantial numbers of men. For this reason government force is absolutely essential in effecting any substantial change within the university; it gives women as a group power that they cannot hope to acquire as individuals on individual campuses.

Local women's groups can use that power, but, in our case, other factors interfered. Many women on campus viewed us with some suspicion, I believe. It's hard to be specific about this feeling, but the professors who told us they had been fighting for women's rights for years were not really much help, either personally or politically. There appeared to be a strain between us and the women from the "old faculty"—the teachers and counselors—who were uncomfortable with focus on research. In part, it was simply the lack of forceful leadership, for the women's group was dominated by a counseling approach that may be good for long-range education but is not particularly effective for political drive. We were left, then, to run our own show, and we did it as best we could, with whatever help we could pick up, but it was exhausting and consumed much of our time for an entire year, 1976–77.

In the first two years (1974–76), we could have used help in gathering data on institutional patterns. We could have used a group of faculty women as our advocates. We could have used help in getting our stories into the local media. We could have used contacts in area groups and some direction to political allies. We could have used social invitations to help us relax and to break the isolation we lived in. And we could have used national reports on professionals who were married women with children and reports on part-time work, but these matters are only beginning to be studied.

For those two years Shirley Graham and I worked alone, in isolation. We found our social lives vanishing as we became an embarrassment, and our souls tightened to withstand the skepticism around us. We stood in courtrooms alone while a barrage of administrators filed in with their lawyers, casting their resentment around them. University people studiously avoided talking about the case with us or told us they didn't "get involved in politics."

As those two years went by, I continued to teach the selected excerpts from *Paradise Lost* in the sophomore survey and ironically read the devils' council in hell with its analysis of political types. I choked, again and again, when Milton spoke: "And I alone with evil tongues surrounded / With evil tongues surrounded, I alone . . . ," I learned what exile was and read Dante, that other loser, when the going got too rough. When I told my students about the value of a humanist education, I spoke from experience, too, for Dante and Milton sustained my fears and enabled me to keep going. They had survived much more; I could do this small thing.

But we were not entirely alone—Royalists or Roundheads, Guelfs or Ghibbelines. Ours was only a metaphorical war, like that between the Tates. And we had help from our closest friends at other universities in the form of personal and public testimony. Individual sympathizers at the university saw that we received relevant documents. And we had the advantage of being co-complainants. For three years, we talked to each other almost every day, exchanged the roles of weak or strong as the battle progressed, sustaining each other. We collected data, analyzed statistics. We traded invitations and excursions with our children, who became good friends, too. Our complaints first grew into an alliance and then into the sort of friendship that comes only when you walk through fire together. We are proud of each other; we kept each other going.

In the end, affirmative action is not simply a woman's battle. A change in the definition "woman" shifts all the other relationships in society. Such shifts quite clearly appear in Western history in the twelfth century and again in the nineteenth when a variety of social causes created major changes. Technology now enables us to control birth and infant survival, those central facts of women's biological life. Given that control, we inevitably have a new vision of marriage and the family, a vision that influences the available work force. Marriage is different for our generation, but we are caught in the middle of new patterns only now emerging. Some men and women welcome the change while others resent or fear it. This social tension accounts for the hostility we encountered in a monolithic university world that lumbers like a dinosaur toward the future. A hundred years ago, Oxford dons had to be celibate; nowadays, American professors are expected to be men or, at least, celibate women.

Will we win at this university? I don't know. Some things have changed because of us. There's a part-time policy pending; it's probably inadequate, but it would never have been introduced without us. The women's issue has arrived at this place finally and forcefully, and the men can no longer pay mere lip service to it. The women's group has been formed; time will tell whether it will grow stronger. The ripples of our action have spread to nearby institutions. The union and the faculty senate had to face the issue and take the criticism their support or lack of support brought them from their colleagues. And we did all this in the middle of administrative chaos and economic cutbacks.

Was it worth it? Well, yes. Like death and dying, you learn a great deal from it. You lose friends, and you make friends and gain enemies. We might be permanently unemployable in our profession. No one seems in a hurry to offer us jobs, but then I didn't get many job offers before, either. The last time someone wanted to hire my husband and talked about a part-time job for me, I said no. And, yes, I still believe in merit and excellence, but I think the profession needs a little more of that old virtue, *caritas*, untranslatable as the word is. Loving kindness, humanity, charity are its closest English equivalents. Would that we all had more of it!

POSTSCRIPT

I have been asked to add a note to this chapter, which I wrote in 1977. Since then, our complaint has gone through several government review processes and moved up the federal hierarchy. In December 1980 it was recommended for enforcement, and it rests in the office of the Solicitor General. Although our research on the university has been substantiated to our satisfaction by the review, the complaint remains, legally, in the realm of allegation until it is tried before a judge. We have survived personal attack, damaged careers, and angry dismissal. Our work still stands and we stand with it—still.

Joan Roberts and the University

Sarah Slavin and Jacqueline Macaulay

Joan Roberts sued her university in a class action under Title VII (Equal Employment) of the Civil Rights Act of 1964 on grounds that the university discriminated against her on the basis of sex in denying her tenure in February 1974.[1] In her suit she had the support of the state education association. Roberts alleged that tenure denial resulted from manipulation of vague and subjective evaluation standards—standards different from and more stringent and restrictive than those used to evaluate male faculty for tenure. Roberts further alleged that this denial was part of a continuing university-wide pattern of employment discrimination against women on the basis of sex. Roberts won affirmative rulings at the state level, with the state equal rights division issuing a finding of probable cause to believe her allegation that the university had engaged in discriminatory employment practices.[2] The university made two offers to settle out of court, but the issue nonetheless moved toward litigation.

A social psychologist with a doctorate from Teachers College, Columbia University, Roberts joined the university in 1968 as an assistant professor in the department of educational policy studies of the school of education. She pioneered the first formally accepted women's studies course on the campus in 1971. She and other faculty women organized local and statewide associations of academic women, groups concerned with affirmative action, women's studies, curriculum development, and the needs of women students. Roberts initiated research and courses in sex role socialization, attended conferences, appeared on panels, presented papers, published scholarly articles, counseled scores of students, and consulted with the public school system on racism, sexism, and class bias. She taught a variety of courses and served on several departmental and campus-wide academic and service committees. She supervised students, including six doctoral candidates who completed dissertations with her guidance. She created and taught four new courses and secured their formal acceptance into the curriculum, and she offered new experimental seminars.

In 1971 Roberts unanimously was granted a second three-year contract, but in January 1974 the three-man evaluation committee recommended to the department's executive committee that her appointment be terminated on grounds of an unsatisfactory research and publication record. At her request, Roberts presented her case against the negative evaluation on 8 February at a long open meeting of the all-male department executive committee. The committee voted to deny tenure, as the evaluation committee had recommended. The rules for tenure-review procedure allowed the executive committee to reconsider this decision, however, and Roberts' supporters demanded that this be done, physically blocking the door at the end of the hearing until a second one was scheduled. On 27 February at a second open meeting, with campus police outside the meeting room, surrounding the building and neighboring area, the committee again voted against tenure.

In all their deliberations, the evaluation committee and the executive committee concentrated on Roberts' current publication and research record. They declined to view her research in progress and curriculum development as adequate to meet research and scholarship criteria. They held that works completed before Roberts came to the campus should not count as publication credits for tenure purposes. They criticized the organization of Roberts' vita and challenged the status of various items in it.

At both meetings Roberts questioned the criteria and procedures used to evaluate her. Among the issues raised were the following: Were the evaluation criteria and their weighting consistent with university regents' policy? Was curriculum development recognized as original scholarship? What were the implications of having an evaluation committee composed entirely of men who were not of the candidates' discipline? Why were department rules providing for mutual agreement on procedures not followed? Did the evaluation recognize women's studies as a legitimate academic discipline? Did it give adequate weight to Roberts' work in women's studies? Was the evaluation procedure followed in her case comparable to that followed in cases of men recently granted tenure in the department? Was this procedure equitable?

In pursuing her grievance against the university, Roberts wanted to expose "facades of change" that masked resistance to real change, reinforced discrimination, and continued to deny women the equal status they need to develop their scholarly potential. Roberts' goals entailed exploring social reality, identifying institutional processes that exclude women, assessing knowledge, and constructing alternatives for the future.[3] Roberts hoped that her suit would help to attain this goal by providing clarification of tenure issues. The outcome of the suit had wide impact on the academic world. It also established a precedent for valuation of women's studies. This article will present Roberts' case in some detail and explore its meaning for the tenure system, for women's studies efforts, and for members of academe who become entangled in its briar patch. The authors hope to establish that Roberts' case was not unique or even unusual and that she engaged in an enterprise of far-reaching importance for faculty women.

TENURE DENIAL

When Roberts came to the university's educational policy studies department (EPS) in 1968, both she and the department were enthusiastic. She had published one book and a second book, *Scene of the Battle: Group Behavior in Urban Classrooms*,[4] was forthcoming. EPS had a competent faculty doing research and teaching in areas of current interest in educational policy. It seemed an ideal match.

From her first year, Roberts was an active member of the department, the university, and the community. Her memberships ranged from the African Area Studies Committee to the United Faculty (a struggling local of the American Federation of Teachers) to university committees overseeing various academic enterprises. Roberts also was active in organizing the Association of Faculty Women (AFW), an effort prompted by a 1970 visit by a federal team to investigate charges of sex discrimination in violation of federal affirmative action requirements.[5] Roberts was co-chair during AFW's first year (1971–72) and was particularly active as co-chair of AFW's Women's Studies Committee. The effort to organize women concerned with equal opportunity in higher education extended to other state campuses, and Roberts was active in founding the state Coordinating Council for Women in Higher Education (CCWHE). She was co-chair during CCWHE's first year (1972–73).

Roberts presented many speeches and papers during her years at the university. Additionally, she was active as adviser, counselor, and supporter for her students. In addition to the six Ph.D.'s already mentioned, she supervised several master's theses and the beginnings of a number of other Ph.D.'s. Her work in women's studies also brought her many students from outside the department in search of counsel and advice.

When Roberts was unanimously reappointed, the committee said, in its report, "Joan is in a transition stage in her research career." They stated they "would like to encourage Joan in research interest and to support her in the development and application of this research."[6] The attitudes of these men toward Roberts' work at this early stage seem to prophesy the eventual tenure denial. When her promotion was considered in 1974, she had several publications and almost a dozen items under submission to journals or in the process of revision. She had contracts for two new books and was negotiating a third, books that had grown out of the new areas of scholarship she was developing. Still, Roberts' effort was not considered great enough by many department members.

In January 1974 the evaluation committee recommended that promotion to tenure rank be denied. At Roberts' insistence, a woman consultant was added to the committee. This woman was from outside the department, because no tenured woman from the department was available. The consultant met with the committee, heard the evidence, and strongly recommended that promotion be granted. Department rules did not allow her a vote on the committee. The three men, who did have a vote, rated Roberts' teaching and community service "satisfactory to excellent" but rated her research and publication record "unsatisfactory." The written decision they submitted stated that the tenure denial was based on a review showing that Roberts' "publications do not testify to extended research or promise for such work in the future." It also stated that Roberts' "record does not give evidence of research ability or discipline for professional leadership."[7]

Roberts requested a hearing to rebut the negative tenure decision. The first open hearing was attended by 300 to 350 students, professors, and friends.[8] Those making statements in Roberts' behalf included a male professor from another department who described getting tenure although his qualifications were not as impressive as Roberts', a male member of Roberts' department who disputed the evaluation of Roberts' work, and a number of observers who had only rude words for the whole situation. The hearing had the air of a charade, with dramatic parts being given to some, but the male leads remained stolid and unmoved except in their own defense. "I'm deeply hurt that you're portraying yourself as a martyr, Joan. We've gone all out. There is an implication of double-dealing and a lack of good faith, and I want to see that cleared up," said one committee member,[9] in response to a protest about the committee's decision that two books Roberts had published before she was hired were not to count toward tenure requirements.[10]

Another issue raised in the open meeting was a complaint that Roberts' vita was not quite orderly. The state investigator termed this "serious misconceptions concerning confusion with complainant's vitae."[11] Roberts had included both published and unpublished articles in her list; since she had many pieces in various stages between draft and publication, she continually revised the list. The current status of each article was identified in each version, but the committee members apparently could not, or would not, sort it out for themselves.

Tenure at Roberts' university is granted on the basis of an analysis by peers of the candidate's achievement in research, teaching, and service. Service was not an overt issue in Roberts' tenure decision but was referred to subtly in the context of scholarship in the statement that Roberts did not have "the discipline for professional leadership." The tenured female consultant sitting on the committee formally objected to that statement. Roberts' organizing and leadership ability did far more than simply bring together women with common concerns. As a tenured English professor told the committee, Roberts is "a pioneer mind in the whole women's movement."[12]

The committee's main objection was that, in their judgment, Roberts' work simply did not measure up to the university's standards. "Our negative recommendation is based on qualitative judgments of her work in women's studies," said the chair.[13] The committee found that her work did not show promise of solid scholarly research. An underlying premise in these judgments is related to the quality of women's studies as generally perceived by male academics. The problem was stated concisely by a friend of Roberts: "These men have not seen that Joan's work is really breaking new ground. She's an innovator, and her work does not fit into conventional academic categories."[14] Yet, as the state investigator put it, the department's "central concern . . . is with the research and innovated [sic] teaching with reference to social and intellectual forces."[15] This point is of major importance in the tenure denial and is at the heart of Roberts' complaint alleging denial of "academic freedom in the area of women's studies as a legitimate field of endeavor" and "use of sexist criteria which serve to devalue women's scholarly and service work."[16]

The point most telling in the suit lay in a table composed by the state investigator, comparing Roberts' record with that of others recently given tenure in her department. The table was supplemented with items from tenure evaluation committee reports on the other candidates. The investigator listed in the *Initial Determination* text eleven such comparisons made on the basis of teaching, service, or research criteria. The table showed Roberts' performance to be in some cases clearly equal and in other cases markedly superior to that of the other candidates. For example, publications achieved before being hired were counted for others, and for some, high praise was given for unfinished work, including work of the sort that the committee discounted in Roberts' case (for example, bibliographic work and synthesis of existing research). Roberts' service record in terms of both breadth of interest and scholarly interaction was excellent but taken lightly in the committee's evaluation.

The investigator also presented statistics supporting Roberts' and others' allegation that department and university hiring and promotion decisions displayed a pattern of discrimination against women. The investigator found "probable cause to believe that the [university] discriminated against the complainant because of sex. . . ."[17]

That is not where the case rested; the remainder of the story is one of largely painful, inconsequential detail, except for the probable cause finding and the ultimate outcome. After the first hearing described above, the committee faced demands to reconsider its decision and went through a second hearing. The meeting's conclusion included an attack on some of Roberts' supporters by the police after Roberts' supporters burned the evaluation committee chairman in effigy and performed a guerrilla skit. Roberts' supporters forced the committee to watch the skit by blocking the exit from the hearing room. (Roberts was absent during the burning in effigy and the skit, and played no role in planning either event.) None of these things made a difference. The committee denied Roberts tenure. For some on campus, this was "hearing the other shoe drop."

THE WOMEN'S STUDIES CONNECTION

The university system in which Roberts worked is one of the largest in the nation. Within the system, feminist academics have developed an extra-system support facility of their own, the Coordinating Council of Women in Higher Education.[18] CCWHE is a coalition of organized faculty women's groups at eleven of the twelve campuses the university comprised at the time of Roberts' tenure hearings. CCWHE constitutes a network for informational, lobbying, and even litigation purposes. In addition, it has been crucial to the development of women's studies throughout the system.[19] Roberts, as was mentioned earlier, helped to found and co-chaired first AFW and then CCWHE.

In 1970 Roberts initiated on her campus a course that ultimately became a collective effort by several women faculty from several disciplines, by students, and by community women. "Education and the Status of Women" was the first formally accepted women's studies course on the campus. It was a consciousness-raising experience for many of those involved in it.[20] Collaboration by faculty women in this direction was extremely important to women's studies development on campus. The course was broadcast by the university radio station, giving access to countless individuals outside the classroom. The following semester a second course was offered in which women students took on increased responsibility and provided new consciousness-raising direction. In 1972 a conference, "Weekend of Women in Action," arose from collaboration between women in the course and women in the community.

Roberts went on to create and facilitate a new course: "Sex Socialization and the Status of Women." This entailed the creation of a syllabus and an extensive bibliography,[21] which the department executive committee later refused to accept as helping to meet research and scholarship criteria for tenure. As co-chairwoman of the AFW women's studies committee, Roberts sent out a call to faculty women on campus to develop women's course descriptions, syllabi, and seminal bibliographies in their own disciplines. These Roberts collected and disseminated as a series of projected courses for the campus. She also asked for future teaching commitments to these courses. This in effect projected a women's studies program for the campus.

The original course Roberts developed was designed as a "spin-off" course from which other women faculty could and did move into courses of their own. The development of the CCWHE network had similar implications, providing a wealth of resource materials and academic support in the process. Despite enthusiastic support of many women on the campus, gaining system legitimization was difficult. Roberts' own course was shepherded through institutional channels to formal approval as a course in the school of education. Students could take it to meet a school and society requirement. Other early women's studies courses were taught on campus through experimental and independent course numbers. Their existence was dependent on sponsorship by a variety of faculty members, some of whom were not particularly interested in women's studies as part of their own fields. As time passed, other departmental courses were formally approved, but they tended to run into cross-listing problems that limited the number of students who could take them.

In addition, covert hostility, disdain, and ridicule by many men (and some women) faculty were continuing problems. This was true not only on the main campus but throughout the system as well. For example, Roberts reports that one of the chancellors asked her, "How do you see women's studies—as errata?"[22] A woman in mathematics education noted antagonism as well as ignorance to replies to a questionnaire she distributed asking about specialized knowledge of women among the faculty.[23] All the women involved in women's studies in those early years can report similar anecdotes.

During this early period of women's studies activity, Roberts' activities expanded beyond the university when she became a member of the National Organization for Women's National Committee to Promote Women's Studies. The committee was established early in 1974 by Anne Grant and Sarah Slavin Schramm in recognition of the congruence of women's studies and NOW's goals. In addition to distributing a regular news sheet to a large national and international readership, offering workshops, and producing volume eight of the *Female Studies* series, a resource and organizational guide, the committee promoted women's studies program development and supported programs and individuals who found themselves in trouble with their academic bases because of their women's studies work. The committee publicized women's studies causes, visited campuses when invited, and brought in outside help whenever possible. When Roberts' work brought her tenure trouble rather than tenure, the committee came to her support. It distributed a fact sheet—compiled from primary documents in consultation with Roberts and her attorney under committee auspices—describing the case, sought NOW legal support, and responded to university administrative criticism of its public support through NOW's national newsletter, *Do It Now*.[24] It also called for letters to the chancellor on Roberts' behalf, with gratifying response.

The positive and sometimes spectacular cognitive and affective impact of women's studies has been described at length elsewhere.[25] The danger women's studies poses for its advocates and implementers is less often described. A dynamic feminist thinker such as Roberts is bound to make ripples that grow into waves. The resulting turbulence can threaten to swallow up many of those involved. Roberts made ripples by organizing faculty women in this university system, developing and distributing women's studies materials, and mobilizing student and community women. She was in the vanguard of a women's studies movement that evolved into a full-fledged program in 1975. According to a faculty member who knows Roberts and her work, she is the one person most responsible for women's studies on her campus.[26] Roberts was not on campus to participate in the formal women's studies program when it officially began. She was even denied the right to participate in the planning at the administrative level, despite repeated and heated protests by women on campus.[27] In challenging the academy, she challenged its very ideational structure and in doing so appeared dangerous to the guardians of that structure, too dangerous to be granted a seat on the committee.

Traditional ivory-tower structures and procedures for encouraging scholarship are not amenable to radical changes of perspective on women's roles. Universities, after all, are hierarchical in their practical structures (myths of faculty autonomy notwithstanding) and conflict-oriented in their usual decision-making style. This conflict orientation leads to a focus on procedures instead of on content and ideas and to a continual striving for small increments in status and power. Competition, polemics, and hostile encounters are frequent and to be expected in the course of "collegial" interaction. The academy cannot reform itself from inside its own centers of power. Women's studies, black studies, and the free school movement have attempted to correct the white male bias that permeates scholarship in the academy. The development of women's studies courses and the effort to legitimate this area expose the exclusionary nature of the academy. Such exposure at times has led to a forceful backlash against women who committed themselves without reserve to revitalizing scholarship through the development of a new discipline.[28]

Roberts was one of those who found themselves targets for backlash. She chose to face the problem and continue to work in the area rather than to back down or compromise. She chose to argue her case before the academy. As a result, she was excluded without regard for her academic contributions in research and scholarship. She is not a unique case in this university system. The dangers of the women's studies connection can be exemplified by another case, which also was in litigation, or by the case of a woman denied contract renewal at the university in 1974. The same dangers existed on other campuses. In 1976, six women on one campus came up for tenure consideration, and the three who taught women's studies courses were denied tenure. Initially the evaluation committee was unwise enough to reveal that the university's women's studies work had not been evaluated, but this failure apparently was not enough to overturn the negative decisions. A woman not renewed at still another campus in a similar situation was reinstated when her reviewers yielded to pressure for token women's studies representation.

Except in a few enlightened corners of the system, the situation was the same everywhere: women recognized the danger of the women's studies connection and feared for their jobs.[29] Few women have survived the connection and won job security. Although involvement in women's studies can yield both scholarly and personal rewards, Roberts' case tells the other side of the story quite clearly. Committing energy and intellect to scholarship at the frontier of academic development can also be dangerous to professional and personal well-being.

THE AFTERMATH

Joan Roberts—born and reared in solidly Mormon Salt Lake City, Utah—is the sort of woman who graduates from high school with honors and is her class commencement speaker. She goes on to achieve academic recognition and leadership as an undergraduate and then undertakes graduate work. She has the opportunity to engage in field work and involves herself in social causes. All these experiences are part of her personal psychology. They are inextricably intermingled. They are part of the exploration and concept testing that make up her adulthood. What happens when such a person is rejected by a select but important group of her peers?

Such a person confronts a frustrating transition that is not easily accomplished. At a crucial point in her professional life, she encounters an authoritative, external directive that would negate her accomplishments, that in fact rejects her. What options are available to an adult professional in this situation? She could respond emotionally, with anger and frustration. She could withdraw, repressing her feelings, to seek less satisfying outlets for her ability. Other options exist, however, for a confident, creative individual. For such an academic, the channels are prescribed and even traditional: intrauniversity review and, if that fails, then state review channels and, if necessary, judicial ones.

Choosing the review option is a means of expressing confidence in one's ability and accomplishments. It suggests a belief that exoneration is forthcoming. It also is a demonstration of faith in one's supporters—in their loyalty and their ability to make objective assessments of the situation. Choosing review is not the easiest way, however. It can be a frightening experience. The procedure is lengthy and costly in terms of money, effort, time, and emotion. Only an individual who is comfortable with herself and her history can afford to follow this channel.

We have known Joan Roberts for over a decade and have shared much of this experience with her. We are confident of Joan's ability and accomplishment, and we believe she will be exonerated. Joan Roberts has earned our confidence; we did not grant it gratuitously. Our faith, support, and consolation are small things, however, compared with the devastating losses that Joan Roberts has incurred: job and affiliation, income, job benefits, collegiality, professional stature, research opportunities, and much more. In the end, even after she is exonerated, she will not easily recover from these losses.

It is important to stress at this point that academic women often receive honors throughout their professional lives and display leadership ability and intellectual curiosity. Joan is at one with them. Were she not, the endeavor just described would be pointless. In suing the university and seeking clarification of tenure issues, she worked for other academic women as well as for herself. The precedent established will be useful for academic women who engage in women's studies. In this sense, Joan is neither unique nor unusual, nor is she a martyr. She is a mature academic, basing her case on merit.

NOTA BENE

On 13 December 1978 the university announced that an agreement had been reached in settlement of Joan Roberts' suit. The agreement states in part:

> The university . . . acknowledges that Joan Roberts made valuable contributions of teaching and service. The university and Roberts continue to disagree about the evaluation of the research done by Roberts, and continue to disagree as to whether the tenure decision was affected by discrimination. Both parties acknowledge that tenure decisions are difficult and properly involve the exercise of individual qualitative judgments in the evaluation of scholarship, teaching, and service. Both parties agree that continuing development of this decision, although difficult, is always desirable. In reaching this settlement, the parties acknowledge that these questions will not be resolved at trial.

The university paid $30,000 for consideration of Roberts' release. Roberts has continued her academic career as an associate professor with tenure at Syracuse University. She has served as chair of the Department of Child and Family Studies.

The conclusion of the lengthy proceedings described in this essay marks the end of a drawn-out process of exoneration. In an important sense, Roberts has won her case, although the university would admit nothing. Roberts and the university have agreed to disagree about the validity of her claim; nevertheless, a chip has been chiseled in the university's facade. Today, the university has a women's studies program, with a talented faculty. Disruptions in any political system—and academe must be regarded as such a system—can lead to significant change, although the initiators often cannot stay on to see it occur. The intrasystem institutions that have evolved from the activism of Roberts and others have established a broad protective umbrella over women's studies personnel. Although smooth sailing is by no means guaranteed those individuals who remain in the system, the merit of their contributions is more readily assured consideration.

The authors heave a sigh of relief. We congratulate Joan on her achievement and courage and wish those who follow in her footsteps the best of success. Above all, we remain committed to the cause that Roberts has represented so well. With leaders of the stature of Joan Roberts, this cause seems destined to flourish.

NOTES

[1] This introduction is derived from "Fact Sheet: Joan Roberts v. University of Wisconsin/Madison," in *The Newsheet: Notes from the NOW Committee to Promote Women's Studies* (Nov. 1974), excerpted in *Off Our Backs* (Dec. 1974), p. 3. The authors acknowledge the prodigious research and writing effort of Elaine Heffernan in compiling the fact sheet. Her work has been supplemented with other documents and the history continued to the present time in this article.

[2] Wisconsin Department of Industry, Labor and Human Relations, Equal Rights Division, *Initial Determination*, Dr. Joan I. Roberts v. John Weaver, President, University of Wisconsin/Madison et. al. ERD Case #7400847, EEOC TMK #4-1200, 16 December 1975.

[3] See Joan Roberts, "Creating a Facade of Change: Informal Mechanisms Used to Impede the Changing Status of Women in Academe" (Pittsburgh: KNOW, Inc., 1975).

[4] This book (New York: Doubleday, 1970, paper, 1971), received excellent reviews in professional journals. Published before Roberts came to Wisconsin was *School Children in the Urban Slum: Readings in Social Science Research* (New York: Free Press, 1967).

[5] A detailed and documented description of the events leading to the founding of AFW and its early history (in which Roberts was a major figure) can be found in Bonnie Cook Freeman, "A New Political Woman? A Study of the Politicization of Faculty Women," Diss. University of Wisconsin 1975.

[6] May 1971 report by EPC evaluation committee, quoted in *Initial Determination*.

[7] Ibid., p. 6.

[8] The two open hearings were reported nationally. See *Newsweek*, 19 Feb. 1974, p. 75; *The Chronicle of Higher Education*, 19 Feb. 1974, p. 2; and an Associated Press news release, for example, *Marshfield News Herald*, 9 Feb. 1974.

[9] *Capital Times*, 9 Feb. 1974.

[10] See *Initial Determination*, p. 6. All sides of the issues raised in the public

hearings and references to relevant EPS and university documents are presented in the state investigator's report.

[11]Ibid., p. 6.

[12]*Capital Times*, 9 Feb. 1974.

[13]*Capital Times*, 29 Feb. 1974.

[14]*Daily Cardinal*, 5 Feb. 1974.

[15]*Initial Determination*, p. 6.

[16]Ibid., p. 1.

[17]Ibid., pp. 12–13.

[18]Ruth Bleier traces CCWHE's origins in "Women and the Wisconsin Experience," *College English*, 34 (1972), 100–06.

[19]See Edi Bjorklund, "Report on Women's Studies in the University of Wisconsin System," in *Do-It-Yourself: Women's Studies*, ed. Sarah Slavin Schramm, *Female Studies Series*, 8 (Pittsburgh: KNOW, Inc., 1975), pp. 179–80.

[20]A book ultimately was published as a result of that effort: Joan I. Roberts, ed., *Beyond Intellectual Sexism: A New Woman, A New Reality* (New York: McKay, 1976).

[21]Published in Joan I. Roberts, "A Multi-Faceted Approach to a Women's Studies Course: Using a Little to Accomplish a Lot," in *Female Studies Series*, 8, ed. Sarah Schramm, pp. 130–71. At the time there were few bibliographies and almost no original materials available for general women's studies courses, much less for special-focus interdisciplinary courses.

[22]Reported in Roberts, *Beyond Intellectual Sexism*, p. 3.

[23]Reported in Roberts, "Multi-Faceted Approach," p. 87.

[24]*Do It Now*, 7: 8, 11, 13 (Aug. 1974, Nov. 1974, Jan./Feb. 1975), p. 5, p. 2, p. 13.

[25]See for example Kathleen O'Connor Blumhagen, "The Relationship between Female Identity and Feminism," Diss. Washington Univ. 1974; Joan I. Roberts, "The Ramifications of the Study of Women," in *Beyond Intellectual Sexism*, ed. Joan Roberts, pp. 3–13; Sarah Slavin Schramm, "Women's Studies: Its Focus, Idea Power and Promise," *Social Science Journal*, 14 (Apr. 1977), 5–13.

[26]This discussion is derived from *The Newsheet: Notes from the NOW Committee to Promote Women's Studies*, 4 (Nov. 1974), p. 1. *Newsheet* is cataloged by both the Women's History Research Center at Berkeley and the Women's Studies Collection, Univ. of Illinois, Chicago Circle. See also Jacqueline Macaulay, "The Failure of Affirmative Action for Women: One University's Experience," in this volume.

[27]Documentation for this statement can be found in AFW files in the possession of Ruth Bleier and Jacqueline Macaulay.

[28]This discussion is derived from Sarah Schramm, "Women's Studies: Its Focus, Idea Power and Promise," p. 7.

[29]Personal communications and correspondence in Jacqueline Macaulay's files and minutes of CCWHE meetings are the sources for the description of the fears of those involved in women's studies in the university system. We cannot give names in some instances because the women involved are still in the process of trying to find ground for conciliation with the university.

Not by Lawyers Alone: Ten Practical Lessons for Academic Litigants

Phyllis Rackin

Literary people have an ancient quarrel with lawyers. We take our values from writers like Plato and Shakespeare and Dickens, we know the difference between Law and Justice, and we cultivate a fastidious ironic attitude that has serious reservations about Justice herself. But the modern academic world is more like a corporation than a grove, and nothing at all like Plato's ideal republic. University administrators are often men of affairs, not philosophical guardians; and—Socrates' recommendations to the contrary notwithstanding—women still tend to be excluded from high faculty and administrative office. In such a world no woman should underestimate the value of a good lawyer.

I had excellent lawyers—bright, knowledgeable, and energetic. They were backed by the formidable name and resources of a prominent Philadelphia law firm. In short, they were members of the same corporate establishment as the university I sued. When another litigant, in another state, told her lawyer the name of the firm that was representing me, he said simply, "Then she will win." The point I want to make, however, is that a good legal staff and a good legal case, although they are surely necessary, may not be sufficient.

I also needed friends. In fact, some of my lawyers were friends. The person who first convinced me to take legal action, and who convinced that distinguished law firm to take my case, was a friend— a brilliant lawyer who wanted to help me because she was a feminist and because she believed that both of us had suffered because of our sex. That woman's friendship provided me with an obvious practical necessity—access to a law firm whose fees I could never have afforded to pay—and also with a less obvious necessity—the moral support I needed just as much. From the beginning, my friends helped me in both of these ways. Without their practical assistance, I would not have been able to do what I did. Without their moral support, I doubt that I would have wanted to.

A full account of my indebtedness to all those who helped and supported me during the five years when I was "the Rackin case" would fill this volume. I will restrict myself to two more examples: In

50

1971 I was asked to read a paper about my predicament to a meeting sponsored by the MLA Commission on the Status of Women in the Profession. Many of the people at that meeting wrote to me afterward, offering comfort and encouragement at a time when I badly needed both. Years later, when I needed money to pay my legal expenses, many of those same people sent contributions, along with more encouragement. And throughout the litigation, I found support and encouragement in my own home. My husband is a professor of English and a long-time officer of the AAUP. His whole-hearted support ranged from putting me in touch with people in the national AAUP office (and resigning when they failed to help me) to taking over most of the domestic duties we had formerly shared when the countless, unforeseen chores of a litigant threatened to overwhelm me.

Probably the most important support I received—and the aspect of my experience that has the most direct implications for other women in similar predicaments—came from an organization called WEOUP (Women for Equal Opportunity at the University of Pennsylvania; for a detailed discussion of WEOUP's structure and activities, see the essay "A Network of Our Own" in this volume). As far as I know, WEOUP is one of the strongest women's groups currently active at any American university, and I believe that a major source of WEOUP's strength is its anti-elitist tradition. The woman who did most to build WEOUP is Carol Tracy, who at the time she became president was a twenty-five-year-old secretary. WEOUP had begun, like most university women's organizations, as a small group composed primarily of faculty and administration women, but Carol greatly enlarged and diversified its membership to include students, clerical and technical staff, and a great many more faculty and administrators. She acquired a university mailing list and used it to invite every woman in the university community to join WEOUP. Lesson number one: *Make all the friends you can.* To this day, no one in the administration knows how or where Carol Tracy got that mailing list. Lesson number two: *It helps to have friends in unsuspected places.*

Early in WEOUP's history, before I became a member, Carol had filed a class-action complaint of sex discrimination against the university with the state human relations commission and held a televised press conference to announce it. Lesson number three: *Publicity helps.* WEOUP held weekly meetings and responded with letters and articles in student newspapers and faculty newsletters to every action the university took that affected women and to administrative inaction as well. Lesson number four: *You have to be willing to work.* The tone adopted in these letters was uncompromising but not intemperate or irresponsible, and WEOUP earned the respect, if not the affection, of much of the academic community at the university. Lesson number five: *Think politically.* Soon Carol began to receive respectful letters from male faculty and administrators addressed to "Professor Tracy," and some of us began to realize how truly subversive our organization was.

Although most of the responsibility fell on Carol, and the essential ingredient in WEOUP's success was her genius for leadership, nothing was ever done in WEOUP by one woman without consulting others, and women of vastly different orientations were able to work together without feeling that their own goals and values were being overlooked. Carol was our spokeswoman, but what she said or signed was often written by others, some of them women who did not think they could afford to speak or write openly. People wondered how Carol Tracy could keep abreast of every administrative development and how she could produce sophisticated statistical analyses of complicated employment data. But of course Carol had many women helping her. WEOUP grew strong because it reached out to include all sorts of women. Women who had achieved success within the system kept us well informed and prudent. Women who had been exploited and rejected by the system kept us honest and courageous. And Carol kept us all together.

The lesson, in case anyone has forgotten, is that *sisterhood is powerful.*

During the year WEOUP was being formed, I was engaged in what is called "working through the established channels," attempting to secure redress of my grievances by appeals to various university committees and officials and the AAUP. Any woman who has tried that route knows how far I got. Finally, in the summer of 1971, I moved timidly beyond the academic threshold and filed a complaint with the state human relations commission. But, as we have all heard by now, "these things take time," and as the months passed I made little progress; indeed, I had a growing suspicion that progress was impossible.

Then I met Carol Tracy and joined WEOUP. I needed WEOUP badly, needed the opportunity to work on a regular basis with other women who wanted the same things I wanted and suffered from the same conditions I wanted to change. And I needed practical help as well as emotional support, but I was afraid to ask for it, for I had already learned not to ask people for more help than they are willing to give. If they have to refuse, they will need reasons, for themselves if not for you. And the reasons they discover will have to support the proposition that you are not really worthy of the help you have asked for. Lesson number six (or maybe this is number one): *Don't expect too much too soon.*

My lawyers, however, hoped that WEOUP would raise money to help with the out-of-pocket costs of our litigation, which were mounting up at a furious rate. WEOUP did raise money—thousands of dollars—but that was only the beginning. WEOUP needed me too, as a visible sign that affirmative action was not working at our university. Lesson number seven: *You probably have something to offer in return for the support you need.* "But what about the Rackin case?" became a predictable refrain in WEOUP negotiations with university officials about other issues affecting women. This specific reference was useful to the negotiators because it provided a good response to the impressive generalizations behind which administrators often retreat when they are challenged. And it was useful to me because it prevented the university from burying my problems—and me with them.

Some women in WEOUP possessed extraordinary political skills, and they helped all of us to develop the strategy and tactics necessary for survival in a complicated, male-dominated academic organization. I learned from them that the battle I had to fight was as much political as it was legal and financial. They put their political skills to work in my behalf, almost always behind the scenes and often without my knowledge. But, like the good politicians they are, they also knew the value of good publicity. One of the ways Carol Tracy built WEOUP's strength was by cultivating good relationships with the staffs of the university and city newspapers. After WEOUP undertook to support my case, frequent references to it appeared in the press. Although I followed my lawyers' instructions to avoid making any statements to reporters, other members of WEOUP were not bound by the same restriction. This press coverage helped in a number of ways.

At one point, the student newspaper published excerpts from my personnel records, which had been filed with the court. When the other side labeled these excerpts a biased and misleading selection, WEOUP undertook to publish all the available documents in a special supplement to *Almanac*, the university's journal of record, where their authenticity could not be questioned. *Almanac* is sent to every faculty member, administrator, and trustee of the university, so all of them received copies of these documents, along with an introductory essay which linked my problems to issues of faculty rights that might be denied to men as well as women. This brilliant essay, incidentally, was one of many anonymous productions of the best writer I have met in eighteen years on the university campus. Lesson number eight: *People who cannot support you openly may still be some of your best allies. Cherish and protect them.* That publication—the documents and the introduction—was probably our watershed, for after it appeared, university sentiment moved in our favor and created a climate in which responsible administrators could devise a satisfactory settlement. Lesson number nine: *Most administrators don't really like lawsuits, but you have to create a situation that helps them realize that settlement is in their best interest as well as yours.*

None of this was as easy as it sounds in the telling, and none of it could have been accomplished without tremendous expenditure of time, effort, skill, and money. The question of publishing the documents in *Almanac*, for instance, was the subject of debate in the Senate Advisory Committee for the better part of a year, and our side could easily have lost that debate if the women and their male allies had not been alert, prudent, and endlessly determined.

As a last-minute maneuver, after publication had been approved in principle, our opponents, ever resourceful, demanded that WEOUP pay for the printing costs in advance. Our plan had been that the publication would elicit contributions that could be used to pay for the printing, since most of our funds were going for legal costs. This last-minute requirement meant that we had to raise fifteen hundred dollars in one week or else give up what we had fought for a year to obtain. It also meant that we might have to give the impression of financial weakness to our opponents. As we had learned, most of the weapons in a legal battle cost money—prodigious amounts of money—and we wondered whether this demand was, among other things, a stratagem designed to test whether we had the money to sustain the legal battle to the end.

Within three days, WEOUP raised the fifteen hundred dollars—in cash. One woman simply and cheerfully produced her only reserve fund—two hundred dollars she had been given to use if she ever needed to fly across country to her family in an emergency. Others gave what they could, and publication went forward as scheduled. Some of our adversaries began to mutter that money was no object to these women, and we did our best to cultivate that impression. Lesson number ten: *Everything costs money.*

Not every effort during those five long years produced such dramatic results. Some, in fact, produced no results at all. Opposing a powerful institution is a demanding project, requiring not only money but time and patience and perseverance as well. For example, when my attorneys finally obtained the faculty salary and promotion data they needed, after many agonizing delays, the data were in a form that was almost unusable. We learned that it would take hundreds of hours to tabulate the information and put it into a form that our statisticians could use. We were also facing rapidly approaching court deadlines. A group of faculty women and two men spent bleary-eyed nights at a dining-room table, transferring nearly illegible notations from the hundreds of sheets of paper the university had finally produced to neatly organized stacks of index cards.

One point of all this reminiscence is to reaffirm the lesson of sisterhood—that we will all have to support each other if we mean to survive and prosper in a world where being a woman is still a disadvantage. So sisterhood is still powerful. The kind of cooperative effort and shared skills and resources I have described here can achieve results that would be impossible for any of us working alone.

My final point is for other litigants. People keep saying, "It must have been hell." It wasn't. To be sure, I had to work hard on my own attitude: I was willing to give time and money and even to risk my professional reputation, but I was not about to destroy myself with hatred. So I devoted a lot of effort to thinking of the defendants as opponents and not as enemies, to keeping cool and resisting temptations to indulge in self-pity and resentment. I could not have sustained this attitude alone, any more than I could have sustained the legal battle alone. But I was not alone, and it was not my opponents or my problems but my friends and the work we were doing to solve those problems that determined the quality of my experience.

I do not wish to give the wrong impression. Our university has not yet achieved the condition of an ideal republic, and many times during those five years I felt like one of the eggs they break to make the omelet. But on balance, it was a joyous and constructive experience—joyous because we had each other and a cause we all believed in, and constructive because what we were working for was more important to us than what we were working against. For that reason, I have not described the details of the grievance that led me to take legal action: the story is all too typical and therefore not very illuminating. What is illuminating, I think, is the way the women at my university have learned to work together and even, on occasion, to secure cooperation from the men who run things.

My own situation now is relatively comfortable. Although I am no longer a member of the department in which I served my tenure probationary period, I am a tenured associate professor. I have rewarding committee assignments. In fact, during the six years since my case was settled, I have been appointed to chair a number of committees. Most important, I teach the courses I want to teach to good students and have reasonable support for my research. So in a way, this is a story of success and reconciliation.

In a more important way, it is a story of continued struggle. Some of the men we work with have learned to respect us, to understand the importance of our goals, and to work with us to achieve them. The disappointments and setbacks continue, however, for discrimination still flourishes in the groves of academe. We continue to oppose that discrimination with every resource we can muster, but we have not lost our optimism or our ideals. What we have wanted from the first, and still want, is not to destroy our opponents or ruin our university, but to make it a better place for all of us (although I am not sure that our opponents are always able to appreciate that point). We still think our university needs to be better, and WEOUP is still working to that end. The legal defense fund, unfortunately, is still required. But although we have learned to practice the dubious craft of academic politics, and although we continue to take to the law, what we pursue is more than legal victories and more important than a piece of the action: it is an ancient, enduring ideal of justice.

I'm Not Shouting "Jubilee": One Black Woman's Story

Gloria T. Hull

Mine is neither a tale of woe nor a smiling story of success. It is a fable for our times: an account of one Black woman's experiences with promotion and tenure, a story from which, as the Elizabethans used to say, many good and excellent morals may be drawn. I was recently granted the rank of associate professor with tenure, and this accomplishment, usually considered a victory, seems to me almost a qualified defeat, not because of the proverbial hollowness of finally "arriving" but because of the dim, ungenerous things that happened to me on my way here.

In my department, I was the first and only Black person to be on the promotion and tenure track. Only three women had ever been tenured, and, at present, I am the sole Black, tracked or untracked, on a staff of more than forty, excluding graduate teaching assistants and part-time instructors. These figures reveal the terrible, although common, isolation of women and, to a greater extent, of Blacks and, to a still greater extent, of Black women.

Furthermore, the field of Black American literature—to which I switched early from English Romanticism and Byron—and my concentration on Black women writers drastically increase the potential for professional loneliness, since no one else in my department has scholarly interest in these areas. Certainly in a place where Gwendolyn Brooks is not taught in most modern poetry courses and Zora Neale Hurston is just a name (or maybe not even that), no one can be found to argue the relative merits of Nella Larsen's *Passing* and *Quicksand* or give an opinion about Sonia Sanchez's "Muslim" poems.

This is deplorable, of course. But, then, Blacks in predominantly white colleges and universities have learned to survive with such realities—and Black women even more so. As a sister sufferer put it, "All the women are white, all the Blacks are men, but some of us are brave." Coping strategies include attending conventions, conducting lifeline correspondences, paying large long-distance phone bills, and living off months-old inspiration.

Personal factors and their implications are also relevant: being

Black, being female, being feminist, having a nontraditional life-style that does not fit conveniently into any of the usual categories. Many of the common bases for interacting on a nonprofessional level with other people in the department do not exist simply because of divergencies in interests, schedules, friends, and so forth.

Of course, I am on friendly terms with some members of the department. Two or three senior professors have read a few of my manuscripts and given me encouragement; a trio of us talk about music and exchange records; those of us hired together occasionally discuss our status and financial progress; I generally share pleasantries or, in some cases, meaningful information in the halls with most people; and we all work together civilly. However, I don't get invited for beer by the men who drink at the local watering hole; I don't become a close friend of my colleagues through our children's activities; I don't enjoy the company of some nice traditionalists enough to have lunch with them, and so on. Needless to say, all these forfeited activities constitute "sociability testing" for the professoriate, form the fence for the grapevine, and foster friendships (that equal sponsorship and votes).

When I was hired in September 1971, I was rather naive. I didn't attempt to parlay any attribute I possessed into extra salary dollars, and I entered the ranks with good faith, goodwill, a cheerful disposition, and the determination of a Horatio Alger hero. I learned how to teach and be a professor. And, eager to accommodate, I said yes to every committee assignment, ad hoc task, and request to speak. I received many such requests, for affirmative action had impressed on everyone the importance of having minorities and women represented everywhere and, on my campus, there were precious few of either to do the representing. Like most young scholar-teachers, I took these responsibilities seriously and, between meetings and developing and teaching new courses in Black American literature (the department had only one lying fallow), I barely managed sleep and a rudimentary personal life.

Later, I made time for research, writing, and other professional endeavors. Thus, when I presented my promotion and tenure dossier in the fall of 1976, it documented a record of "enviable" service to the campus and community, a well-rounded list of successful courses, a number of well-received papers delivered at other schools and national conventions, and a respectable bibliography of articles, poems, and significant work in progress most on the subject of Black women writers treated from an almost interdisciplinary, thoroughly Black, and consciously feminist perspective.

Then, interesting and, I'm embarrassed to say, unexpected things happened, occurrences that I should have been alerted to by these previous experiences: (1) being told at my three-year contract renewal review to document my agreement with my chairperson that I concentrate on Black American literature for my good and the good of the department; (2) getting the disquieting impression that some faculty believed perhaps that Black literature wasn't all that important and that maybe it wasn't such a fine idea to focus on it; (3) not being promoted the previous year and being given reasons that were plausible, yet suspect, since it appeared later that there was no intention to promote any fifth-year person (why, I wondered, were we put through this painful and fruitless charade?); and (4) being told at that fifth-year review to produce more scholarship and to be "ruthless" in chopping off "service" (why, I wondered further, didn't someone give me this helpful advice sooner?).

Even though I knew that some of my departmental colleagues, like the literary establishment at large, did not or could not truly accept and appreciate the kind of work I was doing, I was not psychologically or emotionally prepared for the deliberate misreading, misevaluation, and generally negative attitude a number of them manifested. For instance, because my research was not strictly disciplinary and the analysis I was doing not solely New Critical, my work was perceived as merely descriptive (which it wasn't—but then, what is wrong with describing important material that almost no one is aware exists?). Practically everything got trivialized or picked at—if not simply dismissed. The unkindest cut of all came from a woman on the promotion and tenure committee who apparently did not forcefully contradict the trend or tone of the evaluation but who I had thought might do so, if not from pure feelings of empathy and scholarly appreciation, then certainly from political awareness.

These events are dreary enough; still, in this brief recital (based on facts and my perceptions of a confidential process all the details of which I have not been privy to), I am omitting discussion of points such as how my large service contribution was almost ignored, how my being slowed down by my sanctioned and departmentally beneficial change of field was not sufficiently taken into account, how the predominantly Black and women's journals in which I was publishing probably did not rate very highly on the "recognized"-"established" scale, and how those personal differences mentioned above undoubtedly affected the way I was viewed. As someone remarked to me, "They got to like you"—period.

This entire process literally and spiritually flattened me for two days. I could only conclude sadly that racist and sexist biases were probably operating (perhaps unconsciously) on both personal and professional levels.

Thank heaven that the three evaluations from my disinterested outside referees—all nationally esteemed authorities who were either chosen or approved by the promotion and tenure committee itself— were, as my recommending letter eventually phrased it, "positive and occasionally laudatory." (This, of course, only increases the irony of what went on within the department.) And since this was the first year that solicitation of external opinions was made a formal part of the review procedure—because of a new, progressive department chair— I shudder to think what might have happened under the old system.

Thank heaven, also, that the kind of judgmental narrowness I have been describing was not all-pervasive and that the majority of the committee did vote to recommend me for promotion and tenure. Constantly reminding myself of this fact solaced me then and heartens me now.

Yet, remembering these experiences, I feel much more like singing "How I Got Ovah," a gritty litany of trials and tribulations overcome, than shouting "Jubilee."

1977

The Crux: Quality Judgment and Departmental Autonomy

Marianne Burkhard

In March 1976, after a struggle lasting more than two years, I won my case against my department, on a complaint of sex discrimination involving promotion and tenure. Although I had filed an official complaint with the state Fair Employment Practices Commission (FEPC), my case was settled within the university through the campus affirmative action office. Against the sustained objections of the department, the university granted me tenure and promotion to the rank of associate professor. The resolution of my case set an important precedent: the department's negative decision—finally recognized as highly questionable—was superseded by a decision made outside the department. In other words: the principle that promotion to tenured rank must originate in the department was broken for the first time. The serious injustice of a discriminatory, unprofessional judgment was recognized and corrected.

To avoid a long narrative explaining all the intricacies of the case, I shall limit my remarks to an outline of the events and procedures and then focus on some main points. Theoretically, the problem was not insoluble, and recourse to an outside review appeared as an obvious remedy. Practically, however, the case and the solution posed considerable difficulties because they came in conflict with established procedures that had never really been questioned and required an interpretation of the department's statutory rights that had never before been used. And, as in every discrimination case, a large part of the problem was of a psychological and political nature.

SUMMARY OF EVENTS

In 1973–74, my sixth year as an assistant professor in a language department (with a faculty of twenty) in a Big Ten school, the department decided not to recommend me for tenure and promotion and to terminate me. No specific reasons were given; dropping enrollments and the need for my specialty were never made an issue and were actually irrelevant to my case. Since in comparison with

61

men who had been promoted I had a very good publication record and good teaching evaluations, I felt discriminated against and appealed the decision.

The appeal went through several stages. First, I appealed to the department, which turned me down again. Since no other provisions for an appeal existed at the time, I then appealed directly to the dean of the college of liberal arts and sciences, who subsequently conducted two hearings. Disturbed by several aspects of the departmental decision the dean ordered (1) that the department discuss my case *de novo* with an outside observer present at all meetings and (2) that the college Equal Employment Opportunity Committee (EEOC) investigate possible sex discrimination patterns in the department over the past ten years. The department quickly reaffirmed its negative decision and, pressed for reasons, severely criticized my research and teaching. Slowly and on the basis of a rather perfunctory investigation the college EEOC came to the conclusion that I had not been treated unfairly, but two members of the committee—one of whom had been present at the earlier hearings—dissented.

In view of the two new negative decisions the dean recommended my termination to the vice-chancellor. At that time (June 1974) I filed a complaint with the state FEPC as well as with the campus Faculty Advisory Committee (FAC), which among other business handles all sorts of grievances and was the last available channel within the university. After a limited investigation this committee, too, concluded that I had no grounds for a complaint. Meanwhile, the campus Affirmative Action Office had conducted its own thorough investigation and fully supported my complaint. On the basis of this report the vice-chancellor and the chancellor decided to take the unprecedented step of ordering a new special review of my professional performance to be conducted entirely outside the department and without regard for the department's decision. Since there was no precedent, special procedures had to be worked out for setting up a review committee of five professors from the college and for soliciting three new outside evaluations of my research by specialists from other schools. When the review committee was ready to start its work, my terminal year was almost over (April 1975), and because of the unusual circumstances I was given a second terminal contract.

Having studied my record and having received three outside evaluations, the review committee, in the fall of 1975, unanimously recommended my promotion and tenure to the dean, who, reversing his earlier stand, supported the recommendation. With the further support of the vice-chancellor, the chancellor, and the president, I was finally promoted and tenured in March 1976 against the continued objections of the department.

WHO MAY JUDGE QUALITY?

At all stages of this long process the quality of my work—especially of my publications—was the central issue. But who could or should judge this after the department had termed it inadequate as a whole despite the six outside letters that the department itself had solicited in 1973 and that were described in a later report as ranging from positive to enthusiastic? Under normal circumstances the department is certainly best equipped to assess a candidate's work in the areas of research, teaching, and service, giving due attention to outside specialists' evaluations of publications. Because this principle had never been questioned, it was (and still is) seen as an absolute prerogative of the department. In other words, departmental approval is indispensable for promotion. This implies a total lack of awareness that, in making a negative decision, a department may be wrong, perhaps even intentionally so.

This unquestioned tradition seemed to have considerable effect on the way the two committees handled my case. Coming from other fields, the members were, of course, unable to resolve the quality issue directly. Yet they did not even address it indirectly by suggesting some sort of impartial assessment, which I had requested repeatedly. Reverence for departmental prerogatives evidently combined with lack of sensitivity for the devices of discrimination that were often interpreted as "honest mistakes" and seen as isolated details rather than as a continuous series forming an increasingly clear pattern. The committee members were reluctant to distrust the judgment of their colleagues—lest they might be distrusted in turn? They were unwilling to interfere, or even appear to do so, in matters of a purely departmental nature—for fear of opening the door for too much such interference? The reluctance was further reinforced in that, from the outset, the committees knew how lopsided the departmental vote in my case had been. Despite explanation of and evidence for a polarization in the department, the department's majority enjoyed an almost unquestioned credibility.

Although consideration for tradition and respect for the judgment of colleagues are not bad in themselves, they did add up to an attitude of laissez-faire toward the existing power structure. The powers that be are strengthened while the complainant, powerless by definition, has to work hard to gain even minimal credibility. The untenured faculty member painfully wonders whether it is really only fair to give such careful consideration to persons and structures that are securely established before giving equal consideration to the possibility of injustice and to the potential victim who stands to suffer far greater hardship if treated unfairly.

THE OUTSIDE REVIEW

The obvious solution of the quality issue is an assessment of the candidate's research by recognized specialists teaching at other highly regarded schools. Once the administration realized that the departmental decision could not be successfully defended before a government agency, an outside review was the only remedy available. This review had to establish, on the basis of all my contributions, whether or not I deserved promotion, and the findings were to become the basis of any further action by the college and the university; thus, the departmental decision was de facto annulled. Such a step had never before been taken, probably had not even been considered by the administration.

Although the department was told that an outside review was to take place, it was not involved in setting up the special procedures that charted the committee's responsibilities and ensured impartiality. The department had no more influence than I did. As in the process of jury selection we were allowed to eliminate a maximum of ten names from a list of twenty-five professors being considered for the committee of five, and we each had to submit a list of twelve highly regarded specialists from which the committee would choose three—ideally from those names suggested on both lists. The committee then asked the three specialists to write an in-depth evaluation of all my publications up to that time, that is, a year after the departmental decision. The committee reviewed my performance in teaching and service; the quality judgment lay entirely with the specialists. For the successful functioning of the committee as well as for the whole idea of an outside review, fair and precise procedures were essential. With regard to those who doubted the procedural feasibility of such a review it was important to show that the committee could work without usurping the sensitive quality judgment.

LIMITS OF DEPARTMENTAL AUTONOMY

Establishing and conducting the outside review went against an unbroken tradition of departmental autonomy in matters of tenure and promotion. To be sure, this autonomy has its positive side, and it is duly rooted in the statutes, although they also provide a limit to such autonomy by stating that appointments and promotions are "ordinarily" made with the concurrence of the department. Once the review committee had recommended my tenure and promotion, the department renewed the protest it had voiced earlier, namely that the disregard of the departmental decision violated the statutes. The department failed to note that in the statutes the board of trustees is given a reservation of power allowing the board to initiate action not in conformance with its own statutes.

Yet the crucial issue here is one of statutory rights versus proven injustice. In other words, it is not the purpose of the statutes to sustain a departmental decision that has been shown to be unjust because it is based on something other than professional qualifications. Equally important is the other facet of this argument: if the department were accorded absolute autonomy, a veto power for any case, all the provisions for an appeal as well as the individual's right to an appeal would be mere farce. In explaining its course of action, the administration stressed the importance of these points, and the departmental protests met with no success. At the same time, the administration's commendable willingness to act seems clearly linked to the fact that the university was under the pressure of a complaint that could have jeopardized federal funds.

In conclusion, this case stresses the following points: the principle of departmental autonomy needs a new interpretation in the light of discrimination cases of all sorts; outside reviews should be required and should be a recognized means of negotiation done by either appeals committees or affirmative action offices; and for the present (still rather imperfect) state of affairs pressure from government agencies is needed.

Fighting for Tenure:
A Bittersweet Victory

Carole Rosenthal

As a little girl, I loved action games, disdaining dolls for baseball and cowboys, tucking a plastic pistol into my blue jeans when I went out. In my imagination, I stalked my way to the ten-gallon showdown on the sidewalk. But in reality, when I played with the boys—that is, when the boys let me play with them at all—the game ritually ended with someone running home, nose battered, face slimed with tears. Those boys just loved to fight! Or if they didn't love it, at least they'd been trained to expect it, and they knew how to hold their ground; acts of aggressive opposition defined them, both to each other and to themselves, ordering them into loose social hierarchies. Fighting honed the boys into "men" in preparation for the competitive future. But for me, as a girl, fighting meant potential humiliation. Whatever I did, I felt caught in a bind. For one thing, I didn't believe I could win, because I wasn't strong enough, a conviction that naturally undermined any innate and lurking urge I had to go for the jugular. For another, raucous and conspicuous combat meant giving up certain public and private fantasies about my own femininity. Didn't the damsel in distress, the beautiful victim in fairy tales, find her way to happiness through being weak? And even when I won, which, because of my ambivalence, was rarely, guilt and secret speculation about what would happen to me later paralyzed me for days. Still, I knew that if I wanted to play with the boys I had to be able to fight back.

Unfortunately, my dilemmas as a grown-up academic woman teaching in a male-dominated college did not turn out to be very different from those I faced as a child. I loved being a teacher, but the long-standing gentlemen's-club tradition was the same old boys' game.

My tenure nomination was turned down by the board of trustees, after I'd taught at the college for eight years. My evaluations and other qualifications were excellent; I was only the second woman in the long history of my department ever recommended for tenure. Although the newly formed Affirmative Action Committee had cited my school for severe imbalances in hiring and promoting women and minorities, legally tortuous prose in the letter denying tenure explained that I was being let go "because of enrollment implications due to impairment of program flexibility since this tenured appointment would create 79% tenure in the Division's full time faculty" and "because of declining enrollments in English and Humanities." At the same time, however, the board granted tenure to a man from my department whose credentials were certainly not superior to my own. No explanation as to how his appointment might affect sudden enrollment projections or tenure quotas was given.

I cried when I found out. Embarrassingly, it was at an ad hoc faculty meeting. Then I went home and decided to fight.

My colleagues' reactions to my decision startled me:

"Don't fight! You can't possibly win."

"If you take your case to court, you'll ruin your academic reputation and no other school will ever want you. Do you want to be labeled as a troublemaker?"

"I don't know why you're taking this so personally, Carole. They didn't say that you were bad, only that somebody else was better. Things are tight economically, you know?"

Others implied with raised eyebrows that I was an opportunist, introducing the women's issue to hide my own deficiencies. I heard all sorts of admonitions. And an academic administrator I'd counted on, who had written glowing letters of recommendation for me and given me strong personal support, told me that he was worried about my mental health when I asked him to sign a faculty petition two women in my department had circulated in my behalf: "The way you're hurling your energy into reversing the board's decision is manic, absolutely manic. I think you're—how shall I put it— overinvested in this fight. You've lost your sense of objectivity."

Not only was I being dismissed from the job I had worked long and hard for, but I was regarded as neurotic for fighting to keep that job. And around the edges of those unflattering judgments, glimmering like TV afterglow, that peculiarly American Horatio Alger success ethic hovered: good work is always rewarded; if a person is not rewarded, that person did not do good work.

My initial rush of activity subsided. My research into employment patterns, my strategy planning with friends and colleagues, and my self-confidence were replaced by inertia. Self-doubt bloomed, then festered. Every less-than-perfect thing I had done in my life, every act I suspected someone else could consider less than perfect, floated on the mire of my consciousness. I wondered if I should just start thinking of a whole new career, forget the whole idea of battling for my rights.

The lifeline out of this swampland of self-deprecation was an abrupt realization that my depression had political as well as psychological significance. A docile, self-blaming woman is far easier to deal with than one activated to opposition by anger and logic. By internalizing judgments and social values that I did not even believe or respect myself, by trying to be a good girl who would incur nobody's wrath or harsh evaluation, by restraining my anger at being denied what I deserved because expressing anger was regarded as impolite or inappropriate or unfeminine or unprofessional, I ended up turning my anger inward, against myself. Those strong feelings that were triggered when my tenure nomination was turned down brought back myths and memories, particularly when I saw others around me, all white men that year, being welcomed to tenure while the door was closing on my face.

Suddenly I remembered my grandmother sitting with a mound of washed but unpeeled potatoes in her lap, her knuckles swollen with old age and hard work, bragging to me in a lyrical sing-song about how brilliant my cousin Morton, the pharmacy student, was and how brilliant my cousin Earl, the bank teller, was and how brilliant my cousin Wayne, who was still in eighth grade, would be, telling me how much pleasure could be derived by the family from the achievements of a grandchild's life. "Some people think I'm brilliant, too, grandma," I said, perfectly serious, eager for inclusion in her litany. I was seventeen, just getting ready to start college, dreaming of great ideas, heroic struggles, bold intellectual victories, and enormous rewards. "I won a lot of prizes in high school, you know." She laughed and laughed. She laughed so hard she hurt my feelings, so hard her legs turned streaky and purple from pressing together and her face grew furrowed and tears fell onto her breast, until finally she accused me of trying to give her a heart attack by saying such a funny thing.

If I now allowed myself so many years later to accept other people's verdicts of my worth, verdicts that I believed sexist and wrong, that were in direct contradiction to my own feelings and experience and that crowded out genuine self-assessment as surely as if I'd swallowed my detractors and invited them inside of me to catcall and boo, I was continuing a long and ignoble tradition of passing self-doubt along from one female generation to another. This is a tradition that women have been bullied into perpetuating. My depression resulted from internalizing social opinion, and it served the system's purposes very well. (Better, in fact, than it was serving my own, discouraging battle with the school's administration.) I was, in fact, using my own resources against myself. I was doing my adversaries' dirty work for them by keeping myself in a position of depressed weakness, so that they wouldn't have to expend any of their own time or energy on a public fight.

At that point I abandoned my posture of crouched docility. I began seriously to explore legal alternatives, tracking down participants in other sex discrimination cases, cadging peeks at old records, and tracing my way back through ten years of old college catalogs, using a pocket calculator to winnow out relevant statistics wherever I could. To be able to demonstrate patterns and practices of discrimination in case of a trial, I paid particular attention to several things: turnover rates according to sex, faculty rank according to sex, comparative number of advanced degrees for different ranks according to sex, and the amount of time it took men and women to advance through different ranks. Women's names appeared one year, two years, maybe three, and then vanished, by and large. Women were clustered in the lowest ranks; most of them were part-time. Even the one tenured woman in my department was only an assistant professor. I also wrote or called women who were former members of my department, asking them to write to me about why they left.

Whenever I felt too lonely or too crazy in my struggle, I called on a few friends who were always available to listen to me and to help. And copies of letters of protest over my dismissal that students, ex-students, and workers in my field were sending to the administration also cheered my soul. There were rave reviews, pertinent questions, and masterpieces of indignation. One was an ironic suggestion to the president of the board that a sex change operation might be the ultimate credential I needed to obtain tenure.

Determined to work through as many channels as possible, I filed two separate grievances within the school. I directed one to the Affirmative Action Committee. It became bogged down in procedural discussions for most of the following year, however, because I was their first case. The other grievance went through the school's excellent union, where I received full support from the leaders, who eventually went so far as to file for arbitration.

Finally I went to the state attorney general's office to request that the state sue the school for sex and race discrimination. Two other faculty members went with me. One had been the only black up for tenure with me. He, too, had been turned down, despite a wealth of excellent credentials. The other was a part-time instructor who'd been refused full-time employment. We presented extensive documentation of our case. After we had suffered through several lip-biting weeks, an assistant attorney general called us to say that the civil rights division of the attorney general's office had accepted our case as a class action. The school was now under official investigation by the state. I was elated and relieved, too, as if I had at last been granted permission to fight, permission that I was embarrassed to discover I still wanted, a damnable knee-jerk reaction that resulted from years of trying so hard to be "good."

The case was a strong one. The assistant attorney general was dedicated and thorough and spent a lot of time counseling me on aspects of the investigation's progress. Moreover, an action by the attorney general's office carried clout greater than that of a private action or a slow-moving regulatory agency investigation, and public relations machinery helped ensure that suits originating with the attorney general became news.

But this period of strong support initiated a war of nerves. The investigations were kept secret on campus, and the fight dragged out agonizingly. I couldn't figure out the school's tactics. Whereas earlier all my adrenalin had surged into the fighting impulse, tensing me for combat, now that I was in a more offensive position, I yearned to wrench my mind away from the struggle. I was exhausted. The school had begun a series of delays, arranging discussion dates with the attorney general's office, then changing those dates, requesting an extension, another extension, then another. One week a settlement seemed likely; the next week it was out of the question, absolutely not: the school would never back down on my case. Spring approached, then arrived with a sudden blaze of forsythia. My final semester of teaching was nearly over. Almost a year had elapsed since I first received notice of my termination.

At a union grievance hearing, the provost, a former chairman of my department who had supported my tenure on paper, denied the charge that I was only the second woman in the department to be recommended for tenure. Although there was no record of it, he remembered "clearly" that one woman had been "considered" for tenure in 1948 and another in 1952. If the first "hadn't left" and the second "hadn't gone to another school," he was certain they would have received tenure, he said.

"The key word is 'recommended,'" the union grievance representatives said. "Was either of those women recommended for tenure?"

"Well, no," the provost admitted.

Not surprisingly, the president turned down my union appeal. The administration refused to reinstate me. Up to that point, I had squirreled away in some deep recess of my stupid heart a small and secret stash of hope that the administration would realize that it was making a mistake, that it was getting rid of one of the best teachers in the English department. My belief that right would be rewarded was that deeply ingrained. But now I had to face the fact that right and wrong were, to a large extent, beside the point, and had been all along. From here on, the eventual outcome depended on who could marshal more pertinent facts, better strategy, and greater power.

"If we don't settle and have to go to court, it could take . . . oh, two or three more years," the assistant attorney general told me.

The pain of waiting invaded my sleep. I dreamed of students who'd earned low grades from me joining with school officials, rising up over me like balloons; I dreamed of an administrator seducing me, promising to take care of me if I would just lie down. Win or lose, who cared about teaching at that school anymore? Who cared about academic integrity or equal rights or economic survival? I just wanted the tension to end.

Still, something else was happening. Other women wanted to join the suit. Two women from my department visited the attorney general's office; another called, still hesitant. And I was questioned closely by many more: "What can I lose if I sue?" they asked. "How can I help?" This was a change in attitude, in self-perceptions. The shift from the belief that this was "my problem" to the strengthening knowledge that this was "our problem" marked a definite change in the consciousness of many women. Months earlier, when word of my tenure denial had gone out, the tremendous rush of strong support I'd received from women colleagues had been coupled with frightened ambivalence. Painful to me at the time, the ambivalence had been expressed in confusing ways: in accusations that I was somehow to blame for being let go ("You didn't play your cards right, Carole. You didn't team-play on committees the way men do, and you were too conspicuous as a woman!"); in protestations of helpless femininity ("I feel awful for you, but there's nothing I can do. It could happen to me, too!"); and in a terror of being identified (one letter came from a woman faculty member who not only wouldn't mention sex discrimination "because the board's simply not interested in it" but who also concealed her female identity by signing her initials rather than her first name).

Now, a lot of people were realizing that women could not be inconspicuous. As women we were conspicuous, overtly female, subject to specific stereotypes, expectations, and attributions. We were not male, and thus we were all lumped into the same category: women. Statistics at the school showed that being female made a difference. Not only were there many fewer women but their job ranks were lower, and their pay was often less than men's. Women cannot hide their gender, nor can they change it. We can change only the implications of what it means to be a woman in the working world, by working together, by standing up for our rights.

The attorney general's office sent publicity releases to the press. Over coffee one morning, I picked up a newspaper and read this headline: STATE ATTORNEY GENERAL . . . ANNOUNCES [SCHOOL] SUED FOR SEX AND RACE DISCRIMINATION. Other newspapers proclaimed the story. So did the network news. I was relieved that the lid was off and apprehensive about reactions from male faculty. Nobody on campus said a word. Was this the unthinkable—or perhaps only the unspeakable? At the same time, the assistant attorney general was building a painstaking case, setting fact after fact into place. Legal and public pressures mounted.

One afternoon, as I was making up final exams—my final final exams at the school if my tenure denial wasn't recalled—the phone rang.

"The school wants to settle out of court," the assistant attorney general told me, excited. She outlined the terms. Everything that we'd originally wanted, we would get, she said. The two of us who had been denied tenure would be reinstated, with tenure. The part-time instructor would receive a full-time appointment. All hiring and firing, all promotion and tenure at the school would be under review by the attorney general's office for the next five years. Special committees would be set up in each school for recruiting women, blacks, and minority members for the faculty.

"What do we have to do?"

"Drop the charges," she said. "That's it."

I paused, wondering why I didn't feel more exultant. Hadn't I just as good as won? "All right," I said. "That's great!" I thanked her profusely for her magnificent job—a year's worth of effort that had culminated in victory. "Yes, that's great!" I said. Other women and minorities would benefit from our fight.

We congratulated each other. In fact, after all the energy we'd expended in this fight, we congratulated each other more than once.

Ultimately, of course, the victory was bittersweet. Although I was eventually promoted to associate professor, and although in 1979 a woman was appointed dean of liberal studies, most of the women in my department remain in the part-time ranks. Caught in a shrinking department, their chances of promotion to full-time are now slim. Certainly my victory was a moral victory, but morality had little to do with my case in other ways. Had I been situated at a college in the proverbial town of Podunk instead of in a large and predominantly liberal city, or had my legal representation been less excellent, or had the school been even larger, with greater financial investments at stake in knuckling under, I could as easily have lost. In fact, had my case come before the courts now, at a time when the courts, wary of interfering with academic freedom, sometimes follow a hands-off policy on tenure decisions, I might not have won. Where would my anger have gone if I had fought so hard and lost?

Yet I cannot get away from the conviction that the fight itself was important, that I needed to face up to this fight. I wasn't fighting solely for a principle, or even for my economic right, though both reasons were desperately important to me. I had to wage a battle on two fronts, the external and the internal. In the external world, at the school, I confronted a sexism that was so basic, so casual, so overriding, that it was almost out of consciousness. When I returned in the fall I had to face various male colleagues who believed I'd strong-armed my way back, their shortened memories and their own fears of female retaliation permitting them to forget that my merit had never been in question, that my tenure had been voted on by my department and had been highly recommended by the chairman, the dean, and the provost—the academic officers—before I'd come up against the locked door of the board.

But the war that made the victory so bittersweet was the one I had to fight inside myself, against internalized social images, against the sexism I'd swallowed and believed so long ago as a female child, sexism I'd accepted right up until its Gorgon face terrified and paralyzed me. I had to examine my terrible fears of fighting with the boys, the fear of winning as well as the fear of losing, the awful and untrue notions that defined me. My psyche became a jousting ground of clashing values and self-images, tinny social concepts tilting up against raw feelings, feelings frightening in their intensity. I fought, in the end, to recover my own belief in myself, my own belief in the seriousness of my life, in my abilities, in my experience of reality. I fought for my right to take a fighting chance, win or lose. The fight for tenure was a clear victory. The battle for female autonomy goes on. And on.

Part II

CONTEXTS AND PROCESSES

Career Politics and the Practice of Women's Studies

Sara Coulter

The rapid growth of women's studies courses and programs over the last decade indicates that a significant number of faculty members have been devoting their professional time and talent to a new approach to knowledge of the human situation. Exact figures are difficult to obtain, but Florence Howe estimated that, as of 1977, there were more than 270 programs on as many campuses and "some 15,000 courses developed by 8,500 teachers at 1,500 different institutions."[1] The figures for 1981 would probably be higher. These faculty are typically spread across the campus in traditional departments with a small number in any one department. Thus, women's studies faculty are united by a common interest but separated by departmental affiliation.

For the typical faculty member in a traditional department, participation in women's studies involves a variety of conflicts and rewards, both personal and professional. The primary motivation for such participation is the conviction that women's studies addresses real and neglected needs, a conviction based on personal experience and thus able to elicit the extra commitment, the extra energy, of deeply felt injustice. The primary reward for working in this field is having contributed to the gradual elimination of that injustice. However, inasmuch as women's studies is a significant and valuable contribution to society and academia, participating faculty members should receive the appropriate, professional rewards. They generally do not. Where women's studies is not met with open or disguised hostility, it is, at best, evaluated as a marginal field, regardless of the degree of official acceptance. The radical nature of women's studies mobilizes all the defenders of tradition. As part of and in addition to simple hostility, the values and power struggles of the academic world affect women's studies faculty in a number of negative ways.

First, faculty developing women's studies programs must negotiate with both the administration and the other faculty, but these two groups inevitably have different priorities and different abilities to make their priorities prevail. Largely for political reasons, the administration is likely to be receptive to new ideas and to encourage their development by the means within its authority. In response to student and faculty interest, the administration can make it possible to develop a program by giving the program official status, supplying a budget, providing time or money for administrators of the program, and helping to shepherd the program through the necessary procedures of the institution. Thus, women's studies programs often receive important, initial support from the administration and are later able to create a nucleus around which interested faculty can gather and a means by which they can participate in teaching courses. But the professional fate of those faculty members rests not with the administration but with the faculty, first at the department level and later at higher levels, according to the formal processes of the institution. What the administration sees as important the faculty may view as insignificant.

Faculty are oriented toward disciplines and departments. They have been trained to be so; they are rewarded for being so. Thus, they may view new programs outside their own department and the faculty who participate in them with hostility or indifference. The amount of antipathy depends, of course, on how conservative are the attitudes of individual faculty members and how much of a competitive threat the new program presents to the department (for enrollment, funds, etc.). If the program is of some benefit to the department—if it increases enrollment by creating new courses, for instance—it will be tolerated with nominal courtesy accompanied by the secret conviction that it is basically a betrayal of the integrity of the discipline and one of the more distasteful in a long series of compromises necessitated by the hard times higher education now faces. These feelings surface in promotion and tenure evaluations. Although participation in a new program usually requires greater than average effort, scholarly perspective, courage, and intellectual imagination, when the activities and accomplishments of faculty members are evaluated, the balance will usually tip in the direction of those who have followed the traditional route. This will be true even if the evaluators admire the participants and are not hostile to the new program. Habit and rationalized self-interest will carry the day in decisions that are now based on finer and finer distinctions.

By one method or another, work in women's studies can be evaluated at less than its true value. If the work was done on the basis of released time or if it was otherwise outside the departmental load allotment, the department, with some justification, will evaluate only the work done within the departmental load and leave the remainder uncounted or allow it to be evaluated by others whom the department does not take as seriously. The effect is to reduce the relative merit of the partial-load versus the full-load faculty member. If the work was done as part of the departmental load—a women's studies course in the department, for instance—it might receive equal consideration, but if it is a marginal area of scholarship within the discipline, it is still vulnerable to those who wish to devalue it. Many faculty regard participation in women's studies as a personal quirk or a leisure-time enthusiasm, like raising dahlias, rather than as a serious area of scholarship and a contribution to knowledge. Faculty members are evaluated on their other, more traditional work in the department, with the women's studies element treated perhaps not as a minus but as a zero, rather than as the considerable plus that it should be. Another interesting inconsistency can occur between the hiring and the retention or promotion decisions. Administrative priorities often affect the former more than the latter. Thus an individual may be hired because of special abilities in women's studies but have difficulty retaining the job or advancing because other department members do not think her or his special abilities are important to the school or relevant to their goals. Participation in women's studies, therefore, in effect, operates negatively in a highly competitive situation where no one can afford to have anything less than a full record in her or his favor.

Second, the values of the academic world affect women's studies faculty in a negative way because, unlike participation in traditional disciplines, involvement in women's studies often necessitates involvement in administration. Faculty tend to devalue administrative work when they evaluate other faculty members. Even when such work is done very well and by their most respected colleagues, evaluators see it as necessary drudgery, as a martyrdom sought by few, or as dues to the profession. Interestingly enough, the details of administrative work that are most in disfavor are those that would usually be described as "feminine"—keeping others happy, making it possible for others to achieve their goals, tending to paperwork, doing the housekeeping—while those that are most in favor are those that some would describe as "masculine"—gaining and using power, especially to advance one's own career, and controlling funds. Furthermore, involvement with administration makes the individual suspect to faculty colleagues by placing her or him in partial alliance with the administration, the adversary. If the faculty member seeks a future in administration, then this alienation is a necessary price for future advantage, but if the faculty member does not have administrative ambitions, she or he is spending time (that most valuable of career ingredients) in a manner not to her or his career advantage. In the traditional system, administrative work is a possibility only for those who are already established in their department or discipline and can afford to use their time in this way. The opposite is true for faculty in women's studies. The establishment and development of a women's studies program requires considerable administrative talent because there are few precedents and because it is necessary to work across the entire campus community rather than within a small segment of it. The faculty doing this work are usually young. As a result, the administrative work is doubly difficult because they have not as yet had an opportunity to learn the how and who of their institution, and it is doubly costly in their career advancement, for they cannot afford to have any part of their record devalued. They would reap greater career rewards if they devoted the time and energy to an article or a book. Although faculty in these partial administrative positions can do the best job, the evaluation process makes it costly and may eventually produce what faculty most fear: faculty administrators replaced by professional administrators at all levels.

Finally, the entire system of academic evaluation is designed to reward personal, individual achievement (the most knowledge, the most skill in teaching, the most publications—all acquired by the individual and increasing her or his worth) rather than collective effort and contributions to a group or community. Since much of the theory and practice of the women's movement is collective in nature, work done in women's studies is difficult to evaluate in traditional terms for the purpose of rewarding particular individuals. The traditional model of personal success and development produces a clearly defined record of accomplishment that adheres firmly to the individual, is relatively free of ambiguity, and moves with the individual from one institution to another, inevitably representing an increasing accumulation over time. Contributions to the community, by contrast, are general, vague, and remain with the community when the individual moves on. Women, whether they participate in women's studies or not, are particularly likely to be oriented to community contributions and consequently may not be evaluated justly by a system that places its major emphasis on personal accomplishment. Inasmuch as the health of an academic institution depends on both kinds of accomplishments, it is unfortunate that we do not have more effective means for encouraging and rewarding them equally. In the current job crisis, I hear colleagues saying directly or indirectly that their survival depends on personal development and that they cannot, in spite of their preferences, afford to devote time to program development or similar activities that are community oriented. If their goal is survival and advancement in one of the traditional disciplines, they are probably right.

There are perhaps a few things that can be done to alleviate some of these difficulties. Women's studies faculty will inevitably be in the middle of the tensions in the faculty-administration relationship, but they should not underestimate the importance of winning, however slowly, the goodwill of those faculty whose longevity makes their support crucial to the long-term survival of the program and its participants. In addition, every effort should be made to establish departmental and institutional procedures that are more effective in evaluating nontraditional work. Finding ways to document the results of this kind of work would be helpful. Finally, women's studies faculty should refuse to accept positions in schools that do not provide for adequate means of evaluation; they should be fully aware of institutional procedures and negotiate the terms of nontraditional positions carefully; foresight can pay dividends later.

NOTE

[1]Florence Howe, *Seven Years Later: Women's Studies Programs in 1976* ([Washington, D.C.]: National Advisory Council on Women's Educational Programs, 1977), p. 15.

A Jury of One's Peers*

Joan Abramson

I don't care whether it's Jesus Christ
Himself or Einstein. You can always find some
way, if you put your mind to it, in which that
individual—black, white, male, female—
is a little less good than perfection.
Patricia St. Lawrence
University of California, Berkeley 1976

When Title VII of the Civil Rights Act of 1964 was first voted into law, it contained certain key exemptions: it did not apply to local, state, or federal government workers, and it did not apply to the faculties of educational institutions. In 1971 a number of amendments to Title VII were up for vote in both houses of Congress. They were intended both to strengthen the bargaining power of the Equal Employment Opportunity Commission, the chief enforcer of Title VII, and to extend coverage of Title VII to many of the workers who were not covered by the earlier legislation. When the Senate Committee on Labor and Public Welfare completed its work on the new amendments, its final report included the following discussion of extended coverage:

> As in other areas of employment, statistics for educational institutions indicate that minorities and women are precluded from the more prestigious and higher paying positions and are relegated to the more menial and lower paying jobs. . . . Women are . . . generally underrepresented in institutions of higher learning, but those few that do obtain positions are generally paid less and advanced more slowly than their male counterparts. . . .
> The committee believes that it is essential that these employees be given the same opportunities to redress their grievances as are available to other employees in the other sectors of business. . . . (*Legislative History*, 1973, pp. 420–21)

When the proposed Title VII changes came to the floor of the Senate, an amendment was put forth that would have reintroduced the exemption for higher education institutions. In the debate on that amendment, Senator G. Mennon Williams insisted that professional employees in higher education are "no different from other employees in the nation and deserve to be accorded the same protections. To continue the existing exemption for these employees would not only continue to work an injustice against this vital segment of our Nation's workforce, but would also establish a class of employers who could pursue employment policies which are otherwise prohibited by law" (*Legislative History*, p. 1251).

Later in the debate, Williams analyzed the bill with specific reference to the standards that would be required for educational institutions. Such institutions would, said Williams, "now be expected to conform to the standards of equal employment opportunity as established under Title VII, and employment practices such as hiring, promotion, transfer and termination will be subject to strict equal protection standards" (*Legislative History*, p. 1770). Similar discussions were held in the House of Representatives, and similar conclusions were drawn. In fact, the amendment extending Title VII to faculty of educational institutions contained no special conditions or exemptions.

Nonetheless, a number of university administrators and male faculty members have made an enormous effort in recent years to convince the government agencies and the courts that exemptions for education employees are both legal and essential. Time and again they have insisted on "the positive commitment of colleges and universities to equal employment opportunity and affirmative action" (Heynes, 1975, p. i). And time and again they have added qualifications in view of the alleged "unique" characteristics of higher education employment.

Although Executive Order 11246, as presidential mandate, applies only to employers who have contracted with the federal government to provide goods and services, the requirements governing its enforcement should, in theory, be in line with legal precedents that have been set under Title VII. One would suppose, for example, that universities would refrain from arguing that the disparate impact definition of discrimination set by the Supreme Court in Griggs v. Duke Power Co. had no place on the American campus.

But this is exactly what university officials did attempt during hearings held by the Department of Labor in 1975 to determine whether universities should be exempted from existing regulations. The major emphasis of the testimony was that the merit system, in which criteria are laid out by universities and candidates are judged by their peers, cannot be allowed to bend to government regulation. Moreover, women and minorities could only be stigmatized by government-imposed affirmative action, because those who do gain jobs or tenure, even now, are thought to have "been appointed because of . . . the need of the college or university to achieve a certain numerical result" rather than because of their merit (Bowen, 1975, p. 26).

"It would be to the advantage of those federal agencies responsible for carrying out the mandate of the executive order and of higher education," said Roger W. Heynes, president of the American Council on Education, "if the requirements for and monitoring of equal employment and affirmative action on campuses were modified to take into account the unique characteristics of higher education that are necessary for a sound and excellent educational system" (1975, p. 3).

"I would like to begin to associating myself, and I believe, the overwhelming majority of other college and university presidents, with the positive commitment to equal opportunity which many of us feel so strongly," said William G. Bowen, president of Princeton University (1975, p. 6). "But," he added later in his testimony, "it does seem to me that over time the best protection against discriminatory decisions is likely to come from a combination of sensible policies affecting recruitment, selection and advancement; better designed procedures allowing individuals who feel aggrieved to receive a full, fair and expeditious hearing from their peers; and an ever more widely shared commitment to fair play" (p. 35).

In his testimony, James V. Siena, legal counsel for Stanford University, further stressed the importance of leaving more of the task of affirmative action in the hands of the university. Said Siena, "It should be made clear that matters of internal governance, such as how decisions are reached or how the administration is structured, should properly be left for final decision by the universities themselves. Here again, the emphasis must be on results, not on the imposition of a uniform process" (1975, p. 84).

Siena carries his argument one step further. There are two aspects to the problem, he says: "*First*, who determines whether the goals are satisfactory? *Second*, what happens if the goals are not achieved?" In answer to the first question, Siena says, "Before a university's goals are found wanting, there should be clear and convincing evidence that they do not represent a good faith effort to estimate the probable results of implementing affirmative action procedures. . . . Availability data are too imprecise and the means at hand too crude to make refined judgments on this matter, especially for faculty and other highly skilled employees where the selection factors are complex" (p. 89). In answer to the second question, Siena says, "We feel equally strongly that failure to meet goals should not be taken as evidence of a lack of good faith compliance, but should simply serve as a signal to HEW that the situation might require a more detailed investigation into whether a good faith effort has been made to implement affirmative action procedures. Moreover, failure to meet goals should not 'shift the burden of proof'" (p. 90). The university, then, should be left to its own means and its own goals and, if it fails to achieve its goals, the university is under no obligation to explain itself.

The sum total of the testimony presented by university officials at the Department of Labor hearings and at subsequent government hearings on campus enforcement was an insistence on the commitment of the university to a policy of equity and an equally vigorous insistence that universities are unique and are therefore the best, indeed the only, organizations qualified to act as police, judge, and jury of their own equity attempts. The first of these claims—that universities share in the nationally stated goal of achieving equity for women—grows more questionable with each year as university hiring and promotion efforts are measured against national statistics that show that the position of women on the campus has worsened. The second claim—that universities are unique and thus must be allowed to retain, unchallenged, the current peer review system—is also open to question. But in a number of cases at all levels of the judiciary, courts seem to have accepted both propositions in reaching their decisions. My own case is described in *The Invisible Woman: Discrimination in the Academic Profession*; case studies of eighteen women professionals who filed complaints of sex discrimination against their employers can be found in *Old Boys—New Women: The Politics of Sex Discrimination*, from which this essay is adapted.

An example of a court accepting both these claims can be found in Sharon Johnson v. the University of Pittsburgh School of Medicine. Johnson had been denied tenure and had accused the university of sex discrimination in its decision. After sitting through seventy-four days of on again–off again hearings that stretched over many months, after listening to testimony that filled 12,085 pages of court transcripts, after hearing seventy-three witnesses and admitting over a thousand exhibits, Judge William Knox found against Johnson on 1 August 1977.

In 1973 Sharon Johnson had obtained a preliminary injunction from Judge Knox that prevented the University of Pittsburgh from firing her until a full-scale hearing on her charge of sex discrimination could be held. At that time the university's insistence on its right to unrestrained peer judgment did not impress the judge. In his finding on granting the preliminary injunction, Knox pointed out that there had been no criticism of Johnson's teaching prior to the semester during which the tenure decision was made. In fact, one piece of evidence presented during the preliminary injunction hearings was the previous year's teaching evaluation in which Johnson was rated third from the top among eight department members. Knox regarded the belated criticism of Johnson's teaching as important evidence that the department was creating a pretext for the discriminatory denial of tenure. Indeed, he criticized the department for basing much of its decision on alleged inadequacies during one lecture she gave during the fall of 1971. But, in his final decision, Knox quoted at length from the tenured faculty criticism of the same lecture and concluded that "it was not unreasonable for the tenured faculty to consider this in reaching a decision."

In his preliminary injunction ruling, Knox had found ample evidence of discrimination at the University of Pittsburgh Medical School and had faulted the university for failing to offer any defense for its statistical shortcomings: "The defendant offered no contradictory statistical testimony and did not in any way cast doubt on [the] figures. The defendant instead attempted to show that sex discrimination did not enter the decision of tenured faculty to deny plaintiff tenure and promotion to an associate professorship, and also introduced evidence, most of it gathered after the making of the decision to discharge her, to indicate that she was a poor teacher."

In his preliminary finding, Knox had shown no reluctance whatever to take on the peer judgment system. He even went so far as to find "intentional wrongdoing" on the part of the university for failure to implement its affirmative action plan and "from the fact that the decision to refuse tenure was made without consideration of any criteria other than the evaluation of the teacher's teaching ability from reviewing four lectures. No substantial attention was paid to the plaintiff's work with graduate students or her standing as a research scientist. We also have the subsequent attempt to secure material which would bolster the decision of the tenured faculty when they saw that trouble was brewing." The judge then found "a prima facie case of intentional discrimination on the basis of sex," based on statistical evidence and evidence of disparate treatment.

During the hearings, much of the testimony revolved around Johnson's qualifications for tenure. Indeed, Knox said in open court that he would hear expert witnesses on the subject and make his decision on the basis of their testimony. Yet, after admitting that testimony, Knox titled one section of his ninety-page final decision "The Court Is Not a Super Tenure Committee to Pass on the Qualifications for Grants of Tenure in Colleges and Universities" (Johnson v. University of Pittsburgh, 15 FEP 1516, 1977). Said Knox,

"We start with the proposition that tenure is a privilege, an honor, a distinct honor, which is not to be accorded to all assistant professors. It is a very high recognition of merit. It is the ultimate reward for scientific and academic excellence. It is to be awarded in the course of search for fundamental merit. . . . Such decision by its very nature cannot be made by a court but must be made by the faculty."

Again and again Knox returned to his theme—the judicial system does not have the knowledge or the authority to interfere in the peer judgment system:

> while the court might feel that the plaintiff's research is valuable in the field of medicine and is on the very forefront of the expansion of human knowledge for the extension of life, it is not for this court to make such a decision which can only be made by those who have acquired PhDs and spent years in the field. . . . a well informed decision can only be made by the colleagues with whom the faculty member has worked. Thus, the peer review system has evolved as the most reliable method for assuring promotion of the candidates best qualified to serve the needs of the institution. . . .
>
> The court has little doubt as to the plaintiff's scientific qualifications . . . her scientifically accepted output has been greater than that of the others . . . but on the other hand we cannot say that the decision that her research was not relevant to the mission of a department of biochemistry in a medical school was unreasonable. This is a matter for academic expertise in the field and not for the court. . . .
>
> On the one hand we have the important problem as to whether sex discrimination is operating to the detriment of women in the halls of academia. If so, Congress has mandated that it must be eradicated. Colleges and universities must understand this and guide themselves accordingly. On the other hand we also have the important question as to whether the federal courts are to take over the matter of promotion and tenure for college professors when experts in the academic field agree that such should not occur. In determining qualifications in such circumstances the court is way beyond its field of expertise and in the absence of a clear carrying of the burden of proof by the plaintiff, we must leave such decisions to the PhDs in academia.

The implication of Judge Knox's opinion is that no expert witnesses can be used by judges. Why, for example, should it be any easier for a judge to decide on the sanity of a murder suspect after hearing expert psychiatric testimony than on the qualifications of a woman for tenure after listening to the statements of expert witnesses in her academic field? And indeed, Judge Knox did not stop at the university door. He referred to an earlier decision in his own court in which "this court pointed out that it did not have sufficient expertise to appraise the qualifications of those in the teaching profession whether university professors or elementary school teachers."

What is more, during the full hearing, the university offered little statistical evidence to rebut Johnson's statistics, or at least little that impressed the judge, for in his final ruling he still concluded that the statistics indicated sex discrimination at the University of Pittsburgh School of Medicine. Instead of criticizing the university for these statistics, however, as he had in the preliminary injunction, he now said, "Since the factors involved in determining achievement of professional accomplishment are subtle and subjective, they would be difficult to study by statistical analysis." He also said, "The causal connection between these figures and the decision with respect *to this individual plaintiff* has not been shown."

Thus, even though he described the university affirmative action program as "negative action, not affirmative action," even though he had heard overwhelming testimony from outside witnesses as to Johnson's competence, and even though the hearing revealed that the peer review system at Pittsburgh was, to say the least, not quite free from self-serving and face saving, Judge Knox concluded that "the peer review system has evolved as the most reliable method for assuring promotion of the candidates best qualified to serve the needs of the institution." Johnson's burden of proof had not been met, according to the judge.

In the preliminary injunction ruling in which he found substantial reason to believe Johnson would prevail in her case, Judge Knox often cited McDonnell Douglas v. Green (411 U.S. 792, 1973). The proof pattern is outlined with great care in that case: plaintiffs have the burden of proving a prima facie case of discrimination, defendants then have the opportunity to offer nondiscriminatory reasons for the employment practices and actions taken, and plaintiffs then can offer evidence that the "nondiscriminatory" reasons are actually pretextual and a cover for discrimination. But in his final ruling Knox insisted on a far more substantial—indeed, almost impossible—burden for Johnson when he declared that "plaintiff has not shown by the weight of the evidence that such reasons are so insubstantial and irrational as to serve as a mask for what is forbidden by the law."

In another reference to peer review, Knox asserted, "It is also true that the court should not be involved in constantly reviewing the multitude of personnel decisions made daily by public agencies even though the individual decision subject to review may be mistaken or actually bad."

Since forty-eight percent of all women in professional employment are engaged in teaching, Knox's contention is worth examining (U.S. Department of Commerce, 1976, p. 35). His decision implies that, although Title VII was intentionally extended in 1972 to include those employed in the field of education, the method of achieving equity in such employment was intended to be entirely different from that used in other types of employment: it is to be primarily the concern of the employment system rather than the courts, and the burden of proof is to rest on the plaintiff, even after he or she has established a prima facie showing of discrimination, rather than on the defendant.

Howard Glickstein, who taught at the University of Notre Dame, served as staff director to the U.S. Commission on Civil Rights, and headed President Carter's task force on the reorganization of the antidiscrimination agencies in 1978, commented several years ago, "It is with a sense of déjà vu that I listen to fellow faculty members tell me about the delicate, complicated issues involved in making decisions about academic competence. This was the same rationalization used by officials of the plumbers unions to explain to the U.S. Commission on Civil Rights why there were so few black plumbers" (1975, p. 14).

Lowell Powell, former chair of the Equal Employment Opportunity Commission, stated, "The concept that institutions of higher education are 'above', or at least not in the same relationship to the rest of society, is shared by a large segment of the population, and by most institutions of higher learning as well. This view is frequently held, not withstanding glaring realities to the contrary" (Glickstein, 1975, p. 14).

Higher education has received a hearing before the Department of Labor, however, as well as a number of similar hearings, both formal and informal, before the Civil Rights Commission, Congress, and even the President. This indicates that not everyone in government remained unmoved. And it must be said that, while higher education officials were unable to bring about major changes in the regulations concerning campus enforcement, they have not been totally ineffective. Their efforts have helped keep campus enforcement as an example of the worst possible government antidiscrimination enforcement.

What is more, the pleas of university officials have met with a warm reception in the federal courts. Judge Knox was not alone in his insistence in the Johnson case that employment decisions for faculty must be left to "the Ph.D.'s in academia" rather than the courts.

Before the 1972 extension of Title VII to cover education employees, decisions favoring peer judgment were common. In a promotion case, a northern Texas district court judge ruled in 1971 that he would not override the "rational and well-considered judgment of those possessing expertise in the field" (Green v. Board of Regents of Texas Tech University, 335 F. Supp 249; affirmed, 474 F. 2d 594 [5th Cir, 1973]). Yet in that case Green's department colleagues, "including the then chairman and the former chairman," had voted in favor of her promotion. Only a university vice-president for academic affairs stood in the way. The vice-president later admitted on the witness stand that it was, indeed, true that the university did not pay women as much as it paid men and did not promote them as often. He insisted, however, that these facts did not indicate sex discrimination.

Surprisingly, such decisions continued to be common after the amendment of Title VII to cover education employees. Thus, in the 1974 ruling in a sex discrimination case brought against New York University, the Second Circuit Court in New York included the following:

> Of all fields, which the federal courts should hesitate to invade and take over, education and faculty appointments at the university level are probably the least suited for federal court supervision. Dr. Faro would remove any subjective judgments by her faculty colleagues in the decision-making process by having the courts examine "the university's recruitment, compensation, promotion and termination and by analyzing the way these procedures are applied to the claimant personally" (Applt's Br. p. 26). All this information she would obtain "through extensive discovery either by the EEOC or the litigant herself" (id.). This argument might well lend itself to a reductio ad absurdum rebuttal. Such a procedure, in effect, would require a faculty committee charged with recommending or withholding advancements or tenure appointments to subject itself to a court inquiry at the behest of unsuccessful and disgruntled candidates as to why the unsuccessful was not as well qualified as the successful. This decision would then be passed on by a Court of Appeals or even the Supreme Court. The process might be simplified by a legislative enactment that no faculty appointment or advancement could be made without the committee obtaining a declaratory judgment naming the successful candidate after notice to all contending candidates to present their credentials

for court inspection and decision. This would give "due process" to all contenders, regardless of sex, to advance their "I'm as good as you are" arguments. But such a procedure would require discriminating analysis of the qualifications of each candidate for hiring or advancement, taking into consideration his or her educational experience, the specifications of the particular position open and, of great importance, the personality of the candidate. (Faro v. N.Y. University, 8 FEP Cases 609)

In a race discrimination case brought in 1975, the Southern District Court in New York ruled:

The weight to be given scholarly writings and their publication in a tenure decision involves judgmental evaluation by those who live in the academic world and who are charged with responsibility of decision. Scholarship and research have been described as "the indispensable tools of the scholar's trade," and as such they should be left to the scholars. Absent a showing of discrimination or other violations of constitutional or statutory rights, the court is guided by the words of Judge Moore (in Faro): "Of all fields, which the federal courts should hesitate to invade and take over, education and faculty appointments at a University level are probably the least suited for federal court supervision." This surely is not a case for federal intervention. (Labat v. Board of Higher Education, City of N.Y., 10 E.P.D. Par. 10,563, p. 6335 [S.D. N.Y. 1975])

In Peters v. Middlebury College, in 1976, the judge ruled: "Absent an impermissible discrimination, the federal courts will not intrude to supervise faculty appointments and tenure" (12 FEP Cases, 297–305, 1976). And in Cussler v. University of Maryland, the judge made a similar ruling (430 F. Supp. 602 [1977]).

Most of the judges seemed to allow that deference to peer review operates only in the absence of discrimination, but it is clear from the cases that a great deal of evidence of discrimination was offered. This is evident, for example, in the text of the Peters decision itself where the judge wrote, "Until . . . 1968, there were no full time women faculty members in the English department at Middlebury College. There have been no full professors who were women at Middlebury at any time. There are four women at Middlebury who are tenured members of the faculty; none in the English department." Peters was able to introduce evidence of considerable antagonism among members of the English department faculty toward her feminist views and toward courses she introduced on women in literature. Although some doubt had been raised by campus committee about "the effect that plaintiff's feminist activities and beliefs had on the decision not to reappoint," both the committee and the judge ultimately decided that the effect was insufficient and could therefore be ignored. And even though there was evidence that Peter's teaching was not adequately audited by faculty members and was well received by students, the judge demurred to the peer judgment that found her teaching inadequate for rehiring.

Margaret Cussler's charge was that the University of Maryland had denied her a promotion to full professor and continued to underpay her because of sex discrimination in the sociology department. She, too, was able to bring in considerable evidence of discrimination, including a report by a committee within her own department that concluded the department had been recalcitrant in its hiring and promotion of women. In spite of her evidence, a courtroom exchange on the efficacy of the peer review system indicates that the judge remained unmoved. The defense attorneys in that case brought a female university president who testified that even if sex discrimination did exist on the campus, neither university administrators nor courts should override departmental decisions. Cussler's attorney, Sylvia Roberts, commented, "I believe the U.S. Congress gave us that right." Her comment prompted Judge Edward Northrup to reply, "I don't say the U.S. Congress is always correct. If they're right fifty percent of the time, they're doing good."

The attitude of the judge in the Cussler case was hardly unusual: not only have judges been unwilling to consider sex discrimination a serious charge but they have also gone out of their way, in a number of cases, to malign or belittle the victims of that discrimination. Thus, in Faro, the judge indicated his hostility to the plaintiff by insisting, "Dr. Faro, in effect, envisions herself as a modern Jeanne d'Arc fighting for the rights of embattled womanhood on an academic battlefield, facing a solid phalanx of males and male faculty prejudice."

And in Johnson, the judge went out of his way to refer to the Faro language: "We need not characterize the plaintiff as envisioning herself a modern Jeanne d'Arc as the plaintiff was termed by the Second Circuit in Faro v. NYU, 502 F 2d 1229 (1d cir 1974) to recognize that the case is regarded by many as a test of the rights of female professors to gain tenure and promotion in academia under Title VII. This is regarded as one of the bastions of male chauvinism."

In contrast, in Cramer v. Virginia Commonwealth University (415 F. Supp. 673 [1976]), a case brought successfully by a white male charging that affirmative action had lost him a potential job, the judge went out of his way to express sympathy for the plaintiff, insisting that the only persons to benefit from affirmative action plans were "the thousands of persons engaged in the civil rights business, bureaucrats, lawyers, lobbyists, and politicians." The plaintiff and his fellows were, said the judge, "flattened by the civil rights steamroller."

University claims of good faith and nondiscriminatory intent, as they battle the law in the agencies and in the courts, may convince university officials themselves. By 1976, however, those claims had begun to wear thin. In an article in the *Journal of College and University Law*, for example, Ray Aiken, who serves as legal counsel for Marquette University, reviewed the cases in which universities had successfully defended themselves against discrimination charges by drawing forth judicial deference to the peer review system. He then went on to note that the level of deference was not yet sufficiently high: "To achieve for higher education a tolerable legal atmosphere will require that the attitude of legal deference signaled by these cases becomes solidly ingrained in the total substance of the law dealing with processes of academic evaluation, selection and rejection" (1976, p. 105). Aiken, however, continued:

> At the moment, that is by no means the situation in which we find ourselves. Higher education finds itself especially vulnerable to an unrelenting and formidable attack by public and private agencies single-mindedly dedicated to the achievement of one social or political objective or another; and those agencies treat the broad standards of academic evaluation as largely irrelevant—even hostile—to their own purposes and responsibilities. Armed with a great array of investigative, regulatory, and prosecutorial weapons they have compiled a spotty record of occasional administrative and quasi-judicial victories over public and private colleges and universities which, even if rather regularly overturned in the courts, nevertheless sap both the energies and the resources of the institutions and their personnel. (pp. 105-06)

This view, expressed in 1976, stands in sharp contrast to the statement of Senator Williams that "[t]o continue the existing exemption . . . would also establish a class of employers who could pursue employment policies which are otherwise prohibited by law."

Educational institutions still seek to remain such a class of employers. And with the help of federal judges it appears that they will be able to retain their exemption from the law of the land for some time to come. Only one recent legal decision offered temporary promise that the picture in the future might not be as grim as it has been in the past. In January 1978 First Circuit Court Judge Hugh H.

Bownes found in favor of a plaintiff who had brought a Title VII action
for discrimination in promotion and salary level (Sweeney v. Bd. of
Trustees of Keene State College, et al., 569 F 2d 169 [1978]). Judge
Bownes met the issue of peer judgment squarely, recounted the
decisions that preceded his, and admonished his fellow judges for
their ready deferral to academics:

> However, we voice misgivings over one theme recurrent in those
> opinions: the notion that courts should keep "hands off" the
> salary, promotion, and hiring decisions of colleges and
> universities. This reluctance no doubt arises from the courts'
> recognition that hiring, promotion, and tenure decisions require
> subjective evaluation most appropriately made by persons
> thoroughly familiar with the academic setting. Nevertheless, we
> caution against permitting judicial deference to result in judicial
> abdication of a responsibility entrusted to the courts by
> Congress. That responsibility is simply to provide a forum for
> the litigation of complaints of sex discrimination in institutions
> of higher learning as readily as for other Title VII suits.

The Sweeney case was promising indeed. It reversed a trend that
had consistently plagued academic women bringing Title VII suits
and reminded judges of the intent of Congress in extending Title VII
to employees in the field of education. The decision was the first at
the circuit level in which a judge has been unwilling to leave the
business of overcoming race and sex discrimination in higher
education to the very system Congress concluded had brought about
the problem in the first place. Thus Judge Bownes noted:

> Particularly in a college or university setting, where the level of
> sophistication is likely to be much higher than in other
> employment situations, direct evidence of sex discrimination
> will rarely be available. The Congress was no doubt aware of this
> fact when it extended Title VII to colleges and universities for the
> first time in 1972. The legislative history contains numerous
> indications of Congress' concern for the status of women in
> academia. Statistical evidence presented to the Congress at that
> time made glaringly clear that "[w]hen they have been hired into
> educational institutions, particularly in institutions of higher
> education, women have been relegated to positions of lesser
> standing than their male counterparts.

In its fall 1978 term, however, the U.S. Supreme Court rapidly
moved to nip whatever hope might have sprung from the Sweeney
case. Under McDonnell Douglas, the high court had said that an

individual was expected to make a prima facie showing of discrimination in Title VII cases by establishing that she or he was a member of the protected class, that she or he was denied employment or some job advancement opportunity, that she or he was qualified for such opportunity, and that similar employment had gone to others following the denial. Once a prima facie case is established, the burden shifts to the employer/defendant. If the defendant succeeds in establishing a legitimate, nondiscriminatory reason for his actions, the plaintiff once more takes on the burden of establishing whether or not the legitimate reason is merely a pretext for actual discrimination.

In the spring 1978 term, the Supreme Court, in Furnco Construction Co. v. Waters (46 L.W. 4966), reemphasized the McDonnell formula in terms that seemed to leave it unchanged. But the Court used the term "articulate" interchangeably with "prove" in speaking of the employer's burden to counter a prima facie showing of discrimination with proof of acceptable nondiscriminatory reasons for the employer's actions. In Sweeney the Court, while insisting that Furnco merely clarified the existing McDonnell decision, really bent both McDonnell and Furnco, by making a distinction between "articulating" and "proving," thereby lifting from employers virtually all the burden they formerly bore:

> In Furnco Construction C. v. Waters, 438 U.S.—(June 29, 1978), we stated that "[t]o dispel the adverse inference from a prima facie showing under McDonnell Douglas, the employer need only "articulate some legitimate, nondiscriminatory reason for the employee's rejection." . . . We stated in McDonnell Douglas, supra, that the plaintiff "must . . . be afforded a fair opportunity to show that [the employer's] stated reason for [the plaintiff's] rejection was in fact pretext." 441 U.S. at 804. The Court of Appeals in the present case, however, referring to McDonnell Douglas, supra, stated that "in requiring the defendant to *prove absence of discriminatory motive*, the Supreme Court placed the burden squarely on the party with the greatest access to such evidence. . . ."
>
> While words such as "articulate," "show," and "prove," may have more or less similar meanings depending upon the context in which they are used, we think there is a significant distinction between merely "articulate[ing] some legitimate, nondiscriminatory reason" and "prov[ing] absence of discriminatory motive." By reaffirming and emphasizing the McDonnell Douglas analysis in Furnco Construction Co. v. Waters, we made it clear that the former will suffice to meet the employee's *prima facie* case of discrimination. Because the Court of Appeals appears to have imposed a heavier burden on the

employer than Furnco warrants, its judgment is vacated and the case is remanded for reconsideration in the light of Furnco. (47 L.W. 3330 [1978])

The heavy burden placed on plaintiff Johnson to show "by the weight of the evidence" that an employer's alleged reasons for an employment action are "so insubstantial and irrational as to serve as a mask" for discrimination seems ludicrous in contrast to the employer's burden, spelled out in Furnco and Sweeney, merely to "articulate" any apparently legitimate reason for his actions. But this, at the moment, is the way the scales of justice are weighted for academic women attempting to challenge the peer review system. Sweeney, on remand to a lower court, was decided in favor of the plaintiff. Nevertheless, the legal point remains: the courts have created a burden of proof for academic women substantially higher than for other classes of plaintiffs.

There is no sign as yet that universities are giving up the militant effort to "require that the attitude of legal deference . . . becomes solidly ingrained in the total substance of the law dealing with the processes of academic evaluation, selection, and rejection" (Aiken, 1976, p. 105). On the contrary, the courts have done their best to aid in the achievement of that goal. With Sweeney, which had appeared so hopeful a case at first, the Supreme Court seems to have joined in that effort.

FURTHER READING

Abramson, Joan. *The Invisible Woman: Discrimination in the Academic Profession*. San Francisco: Jossey-Bass, 1975.

———. *Old Boys—New Women: The Politics of Sex Discrimination*. New York: Praeger Special Studies, 1979.

Aiken, Ray J. "Legal Liabilities in Higher Education: Their Scope and Management." *Journal of College and University Law*, 2,3,4 (1976), 3–214.

Bowen, William G. "Affirmative Action: Purpose, Concepts, Methodologies." In *Affirmative Action 1975: Higher Education Testimony before the Department of Labor*. Washington, D.C.: American Council on Education, 30 September 1975, pp. 6–27.

Glickstein, Howard, and Todorovich, Miro. "Discrimination in Higher Education: A Debate on Faculty Employment." *Civil Rights Digest* (Spring 1975).

Heynes, Roger W. "Statement." In *Affirmative Action 1975: Higher Education Testimony before the Department of Labor.* Washington, D.C.: American Council on Education, 30 September 1975, pp. i, 2–4.

Legislative History of the Equal Employment Opportunity Act of 1972, Amending Title VII of the Civil Rights Act of 1964. Washington, D.C.: U.S. Government Printing Office, 74-699-0, 1972.

Siena, James V. "Before the Department of Labor: Hearings on Proposed Revisions of Revised Order #4 As it Applies to Institutions of Higher Education." In *Affirmative Action 1975: Higher Education Testimony before the Department of Labor.* Washington, D.C.: American Council on Education, 30 September 1975, pp. 68–92.

U.S. Department of Commerce. *A Statistical Portrait of Women in the U.S.* Washington, D.C.: Current Population Reports, Bureau of the Census, 1976.

NOTE

*This article is adapted from *Old Boys—New Women: The Politics of Sex Discrimination*, published by Praeger Special Studies in 1979. The book, written under grants from The Fund for Investigative Journalism and the Women's Educational Equity Act Program of HEW, provides case studies of eighteen women professionals who filed complaints of sex discrimination against their employers. It also includes a detailed examination of the meaning of employment discrimination, the treatment of sex discrimination complaints by the various government agencies under several recent presidents and under the Carter administration, and the treatment of discrimination by the courts.

The Failure of Affirmative Action for Women: One University's Experience

Jacqueline Macaulay

PROLOGUE TO FAILURE

In the summer of 1970 a team from the U.S. Department of Health, Education and Welfare's Office for Civil Rights visited the campus of a large state university. The team came to investigate charges made by the Women's Equity Action League (WEAL) that university employment policies and practices discriminated against women. In a style we now know to be symptomatic of what was to come (and generally characteristic of HEW during this period),[1] this team talked only to administrators and not to campus women, who, presumably, could tell them most about sex discrimination at the university. (The WEAL complaint was, in fact, based on a printed study prepared in the spring by a women's group composed of faculty, students, and faculty wives.) This visit took place after the close of the academic year, a time when few faculty members pay much attention to campus affairs. The women on campus didn't know about the investigation until the following fall.

When the women did learn of the visit, they organized the Association for Faculty Women (AFW). This group attracted a wide variety of members, both faculty and nonfaculty, and quickly became active. HEW, they discovered, had confirmed the existence of a pattern of discrimination and underutilization of women on the campus. The team had drawn up a list of eighteen specific and several general recommendations, and the university president had signed an agreement to remedy the problems. The HEW team planned a follow-up review, and the AFW set about preparing for the second visit, documenting the existence of continuing problems faced by women on the campus. When the HEW team returned in January of 1971, the AFW participated actively—and independently of the university administration.

The school's chancellor also reacted to the HEW visit and to the preliminary negative findings. Spurred on by the women's strong

98

requests that something be done about the situation—and by the publicity that the matter received, with help from the AFW—he appointed an AFW member as special assistant in charge of problems related to women. As a result of some strong suggestions from the new president of the statewide university system, a little later that year the chancellor appointed a Committee on the Status of Women, began a review of salary differences between women and men, and initiated a study of the utilization of women on the faculty.

All this resulted in some progress. The utilization analysis revealed a pattern of extreme underutilization of women, similar to that seen nationwide in the early 1970s, and so the extent of past prejudice against hiring women faculty was brought out in the open and recognized as a problem to be remedied. Equity adjustments were made in the salaries of many women. Some women, whose marginal research or teaching positions had been precarious because of budget problems, were promoted to tenure-track positions or even given tenure instead of being fired.[2]

Several more years of work, education, agitation, and the filing of complaints with government agencies by the AFW and others led to further progress. Some day care is now available on campus. Athletic activities and facilities have opened up for women—not as much as they eventually must, but the situation is better than it was. A committee established to investigate equity in granting support to graduate students substantially reduced inequity in this area. After years of efforts that began as part of an underground operation, an official women's studies program was established and seems quite successful, as of this writing. With administrative prodding, a number of departments that had no or few women and/or minority group members now have some, at least in probationary ranks. Also, women are better represented on campus committees than they were before.

With all this progress, however, the major goal of affirmative action for women and minorities[3] has not been reached and may not be reached in the near future. Activist women have failed to make the basic changes in university structure and policy that are necessary to ensure women a permanent, central position in the university community.

BEFORE AND BEHIND THE FACADE

In the early 1970s, women were calling for a written affirmative action plan, adequate analysis of the university work force, significant changes in hiring practices, and so forth, and they began to realize that the university was not willingly going to make major changes. At the same time, ironically, the university was acquiring a national reputation as a showplace of effective affirmative action. In 1974 the woman appointed three years earlier as the chancellor's assistant (later the campus affirmative action officer for minorities and women) was reportedly called to Washington to act as an expert consultant to HEW. By this time active women on campus had come to see something of a credibility gap between the image and the reality of affirmative action. Their suspicions were justified. For example, among the chancellor's papers deposited in the university library archives, I found a memo from the affirmative action officer (AAO) to the chancellor, dated 18 February 1974, that describes her real work at HEW that year:

> I am spending almost half of every week in Washington, D.C., trying to win a modification or deletion of most of the last six items named. It is clear, however, that the most gratifying success in that enterprise will lead to a suspension of only some parts of those requirements. . . .

The six items referred to include listing all vacancies with the state employment service, creating data files on all employees (to permit analysis for evidence of discrimination in hiring, promotion, and salary), auditing positions of the more than three thousand nonfaculty, professional academic staff, creating career ladders and uniform, nondiscriminatory selection procedures for this professional work force, and developing standard, specific grievance procedures. In addition, the AAO described a plan to go only so far in complying with federal requirements as to be able to comply fully within ninety days if the federal government insisted on compliance.

This university has a reputation as a progressive institution. Affirmative action is required by law. Like it or not, General Motors, American Telephone and Telegraph, and the university all have legal obligations to counter discrimination, especially if they want to continue to receive large federal contracts. Why would the university administration, with both tradition and law pressing for affirmative action, offer only the appearance of being a leader while in fact doing little to push unwilling academics into meaningful action?

A number of bureaucratic and political realities lead university administrators to create such credibility gaps. Few university administrators view discrimination against women as a real or serious problem.[4] They view the institution as a meritocracy; yet the federal government pushes them into admitting that some of their most cherished customary practices are not ideal or even legal. Even if they are willing to admit that a less-than-ideal situation exists, university administrators must deal with still another reality: the ideology of faculty governances allows them only limited power to directly intervene in matters such as hiring decisions. To some extent, then, administrators are forced by circumstances to buy off conflicting interests by symbolic compliance that does not incur the costs of real compliance.

Furthermore, those in charge of affirmative action are usually members of the affected classes themselves—minorities and/or women. They can use their administrative office to work for minorities and women only so long as their activities do not incur unacceptable costs to the university. A tacit trade often ensues: the campus AAO in this case came to function as a shield for the university against both the federal government and women's and minority groups. In return, she gained the power to bargain covertly in particular cases where success was not only possible but perhaps desirable in terms of consolidating her position. The following exchange between the AAO and a reporter (R) illustrates this development:

> AAO: I see my job . . . as calling it in the way of the best interests of this institution. By that I don't mean against women, I mean the best interests of this institution in achieving equal opportunity for women. And if calling it accurately temporarily costs me support, that's the price I pay for responsibility.
>
> R: You must be aware of the rumors on campus that you had influence in the denial of tenure to [a woman faculty member].
>
> AAO: What I did was to assure that the procedures followed by the department were absolutely squeaky clean to guarantee there would be absolutely no slipup.
>
> R: Why did you single out [this] case to be sure there were no slipups?
>
> AAO: I would single out any case, particularly where the individual made public statements expecting termination. . . . Any time it looks as if there's going to be an issue of discrimination, I will make sure there is no slipup, no way that we could have gone astray and carried out the expectations the individual may have had. . . .

Then further on in the interview, the AAO says:

> If at all possible I will set a situation up so it looks as if I had nothing to do with the change in policy—that the individual concerned thought it over and decided it was the best thing to do. And to the extent that that can really be the way it worked out—even though I provided some information the person needed to come to that conclusion—the better off we all are.

In short, as any student of organizations knows, the bureaucrat comes to have goals that are distinct from formal goals. Her business is, in part, a hidden business, run with a focus on covert as well as overt goals and often for its own amoral (not immoral) purposes under the cover of righteousness. The bureaucrat, like any other individual, must survive from day to day, maintain face, think well of herself, and strive to sleep soundly at night. This is difficult to do—perhaps impossible—if one admits publicly to lack of progress, if one admits that some problems are insurmountable and that on some occasions one has had to yield to overwhelming pressure from opponents of progress. It is difficult to pursue these goals if one's critics are allowed continually to look over one's shoulder. Thus the bureaucrat must keep critics and potential critics at a distance and somewhat in the dark, particularly in cases where successful completion of the formal bureaucratic mission would involve fundamental and unacceptable reforms in the way the organization runs.

We have not seen those fundamental reforms, and consequently we have not seen substantial and permanent gains for women on this campus. The progress described above is (or was) of the sort that can be allowed without major dislocation of the status quo. The serious failure—or subversion—of affirmative action has been accomplished in a number of ways that can be illustrated by various episodes in the history of women's fight for equality on this campus.

FAILURE THROUGH FADE-OUT

The campus chancellor responded to early charges of sex discrimination by appointing an AFW member as his special assistant for problems related to women. He made the appointment during a break in the academic year. (This is one of the constants in the history of affirmative action in higher education: most moves are made when no one is around to blow the whistle.) The chancellor made his decision without consulting with the AFW or with anyone else, as far as AFW knew. The assistantship was a half-time appointment, which did not seem adequate to meet the needs of a very large university with serious sex discrimination problems.

Similarly, the appointed Committee on the Status of Women was not quite what the AFW had asked for. Several AFW members were on the fourteen-person committee, but the majority consisted of women and men who didn't know much about sex discrimination in academia, tended to believe that it didn't exist, and wouldn't rock the boat anyway. One AFW member attempted to bring up and keep alive what she thought were the important issues. True to social psychological theory, she was accorded the neglect that is the lone deviant's lot. The committee did start a number of projects, one of which led to some campus day-care facilities. However, since the chancellor's assistant devised its agenda, the committee functioned as a support group for the administration rather than as an independent advocacy or policy-making group for women.

This committee met for a year and a half, but in the spring of 1972 its chair resigned, and it never met again. In the fall the AFW received a request for nominees to replace the chair and other committee members who had resigned. AFW responded with the request that campus women elect or name (not just nominate) the majority of committee members and that the committee have "independence, autonomy, and a freedom for creative approaches to the analysis and solution of the specific problems which it decides are important." The administration never replied, and so the committee faded away. It was, perhaps, an administrator's dream committee: it had a few token representatives of the group that had urged its establishment, it looked busy for a while and did a few nonthreatening things, and then it disappeared.

The AFW member appointed half-time to concern herself with women's problems was later promoted from assistant to the chancellor to full-time assistant chancellor, with many duties, including supervision of affirmative action for minorities and women. She then became vice-chancellor at $37,500 a year. She eventually supervised a large staff, but in the spring of 1975 she officially reported that affirmative action matters took only twenty percent of her time. In the fall of 1975 a new acting AAO was appointed. This woman had had little administrative experience and was unfamiliar with the history of affirmative action on this campus. The required open search to fill this position permanently was not done until three years later after a new chancellor came to office. Perhaps the old administration hoped that even the affirmative action office could be subjected to fade-out.

HEW obligingly also faded away, at least until a new era began in that organization in 1977. The report on the second visit never appeared. An internal HEW memo dated 8 May 1972 describes the HEW fade-out as follows:

In the winter of 1971 . . . [t]he staff found sex discrimination at the University at its [main] campus and the school officials were so notified at the exit conference. This office has not, however, confirmed its findings to the University in writing. Draft letters of findings have been brought to me but they had [sic] been so full of generalities that I had to return them for further work. I suspect that the staff did not obtain sufficient factual data on which to base any concrete findings. Unfortunately, whatever findings we could put together at this time would be out of date.

We understand, nevertheless, that following our exit conference, University officials have taken significant steps to improve the posture of women at the University. . . . [The review has] been dragging on because of the slowness with which University officials have responded to our requests for data. As soon as [some reviews of other universities] are complete, I expect [our] next review will be [this university].

But the review was never completed because it wasn't even "dragging on." About two years after this memo was written, HEW approved the university's affirmative action program without any real review.

FAILURE THROUGH ASSERTION OF ADMINISTRATIVE PREROGATIVES

One of AFW's first projects was to put together a comprehensive report analyzing the old boys' club methods of hiring, promotion, and salary setting as well as the attitudes and assumptions that served to maintain discrimination against women over the decades. This report offered suggestions for change and invited departmental faculties to have discussions with AFW representatives. The AAO feared that this effort would interfere with her "delicate negotiations" with these departments toward the same goals and tried to dissuade the group from making any contacts. In retrospect it seems that the delicate negotiations referred to may have been no more than top-down memos on paper and indelicate conversations with department chairs that left them exasperated with "affirmative action." In contrast, the AFW's discussions were conducted on a colleague-to-colleague basis and were designed to persuade departments to accept the need for affirmative action and to help them understand their own practices and set their own goals. It seems now that more real progress would have resulted from the AFW method than the AAO's.

THE MANY USES OF STATISTICS

It has been difficult over the years for the AFW to get an accurate, useful statistical picture of women's place on this campus. My own initiation into affirmative action problems on this campus will serve as an example of this problem as well as of the kind of experiences that provide the grounds for continual outrage among activist women on university campuses.

I was searching for statistics to support statements in a letter that a friend was writing on behalf of a colleague. I was not an active member of the AFW and had not been on campus for the better part of three years, and so I assumed that the AAO could give me these statistics. I called her office and asked for figures on the proportion of women faculty at each rank in 1970 and 1974. I was given the numbers of women in 1970–71 and 1973–74 and was told that the total number at all ranks (including nontenure track) was an impressive thirty percent greater in 1973–74. I pushed for figures on proportions and got some for 1972–73 and 1973–74. They showed that women made up 9.8% of all tenure-track faculty in both years. This did not sound high to me and said nothing about progress.

The support letter was written and in due course an answer was received from the campus lawyer, who said, among other things, "Statistics on the employment of women and minority group members show real progress on this campus, and they are available for the asking. . . ." That had not been my experience, so I started working with data ferreted out of various administrative sources, trying to see if there was progress in any area at all. I ended up well versed on many of the facts that this campus is still reluctant to give out, and I went from inactive member of AFW to coauthor of a broad-based complaint filed with HEW to chair of the group. (This seems to be a common happening in the early days of a social movement: the establishment itself provides extra workers for the effort.)

I found that the apparently great increase in the number of women on the faculty since 1970 reflected expansion of (1) the almost exclusively female faculties of nursing and occupational and physical therapy and (2) clinical faculty and lecturers whose nontenure-track status often represents the discrimination that affirmative action is meant to remedy. As for the proportion of women among tenure-track faculty in male-dominated areas, I found that the study initiated by the university president put the figure at 5.3% in 1969–70, excluding the medical, nursing, and home economics departments. In my search for comparable figures for later years I found many conflicting figures. For example, I had thirteen sets of figures for 1972–73, all from university sources—none matching and none reliable. (In a large corporation, such sloppiness with data would probably warrant a finding that illegal discrimination was taking place.) The best guess, as of 1979–80, is that there are 10.8% women in the group covered by the 1969–70 figures. Thus in ten years the representation of women in these male-dominated areas increased by only about five percentage points. Furthermore, most of this increase is in the probationary ranks. The representation of women in tenured ranks has increased only about two percentage points. Analysis of promotion and nonrenewal rates shows that men had a promotion advantage over women in 1973–74 and that that advantage has not decreased in the last five years.[5] Thus it appears that women are hired into a revolving door at entry ranks at this university.

In spite of this, the university—beginning with an affirmative action report as early as the spring of 1972—has, in effect, been saying, "We used to have a problem, but it's just about solved now." Thus it is not surprising that the AAO informed the faculty in late 1974 that equity for women and minorities would be reached by 1982 on this campus. My own conclusion is that if the best hiring years for women were repeated annually, and if few women were fired or left, the university might just reach parity in 1996. (Similarly, the *Chronicle of Higher Education* reported on 9 October 1973, that parity might be reached nationwide by the year 2000—*if* hiring rates do not generally decline.)

Correcting misleading statistics is a much longer and more tedious process than simply describing the situation correctly to start with. It seems to be true that there are lies, damn lies, and statistics. It is also true that unless you count, compare, and calculate percentages, you cannot know for certain whether apparent action is actually tokenism and whether surface activity is mainly a cover for inaction. This is particularly true for affirmative action where one or two dramatic cases can serve as symbolic compliance with the law while business goes on as usual.

In short, part of the failure of affirmative action at this campus began with the abandonment of the adequate "utilization analysis" that was mandated by federal affirmative action guidelines. The administration alleged that it would cost $400,000 or much more to do utilization analyses. My experience as an unpaid volunteer is that an adequate, revealing analysis could be done annually for a small fraction of that. Some much improved analyses were done when a new chancellor took over on this campus. The administration has not indicated that these analyses were very costly to do, although complaining about the cost of compliance with federal regulations is standard procedure. The data still are not presented in a way that reveals progress or lack of progress clearly, however, and I was still in the business of sifting truth out of poorly presented data six years after I began.

FAILURE THROUGH LACK OF COMMUNICATION AND ADMINISTRATIVE DEAFNESS

Another AFW goal was the creation of salary equity for campus women. This was a major administration project also, and for a while it seemed that it would be a successful one. The AAO devised a method for drawing departments' attention to salary gaps and instructed them either to adjust women's salaries or to justify the gaps that existed. Somewhere between four hundred and nine hundred adjustments were made (the figures vary depending on the source) in 1971–72 and 1972–73. As usual the administration's statistics were overblown, here by inclusion of all merit increases to women over the usual amount. Apparently the administration felt that no woman could earn a merit increase on her own.

The issue faded away after 1973—until HEW revived it in 1977—except for a few nagging doubts about whether equity was really achieved. The AAO made available only campus-wide summaries. When AFW representatives requested more detailed information, university officials told them that the data were on file in the affirmative action office. What the AAO was offering, it turned out, was the chance to look through great stacks of computer printout rather than an opportunity to study a list of identified gaps and departmental justifications or remedial adjustments. The state system administration's figures, using 1969–70 as a base, showed decreases in gaps at all faculty ranks except instructor in 1972–73 but increases at all ranks in 1973–74 and at almost all ranks regularly since then.

HEW insisted on a regression analysis of faculty salaries in 1977–78. The analysis uncovered forty-two possible inequities but further study supposedly showed that only one of them needed adjusting. The faculty members involved appear not to have been consulted as to whether they thought their salaries were fair (although an independent faculty committee checked the analyses). Furthermore, the analysis did not pull out names of people who were paid at the average level for their rank and experience but who should have been paid more, and no adequate analysis has ever been done of the large nonfaculty, nonclerical staff. Fragmentary analyses suggest that great and unjustified gaps exist between men's and women's salaries here. In short, campus women still have serious doubts about whether sex equity has been established in campus salaries.

This story has its parallels in other areas of affirmative action on the campus, areas such as hiring, promotions, and monitoring. The problem here is familiar to any group that has undertaken sustained social action: without the data and resources to continually monitor the situation, without any way of forcing public accountability on the supposedly changing system, alleged success can never be verified. The suspicion then arises that apparent victories are hollow and that observable change may be only surface change, not the structural change that is necessary for true and permanent success.

FAILURE OF VOICE

The AFW represented the initially large group of women who saw a problem in the structure of the academic world and who chose "voice" over "loyalty" or "exit."[6] They saw that they needed not only to criticize and agitate but to make themselves heard—to achieve voice—in the structure itself. They realized that until they managed to get on the committees that determine admission policies, library policy, fringe benefits, graduate fellowships, campus planning, promotions, and so on, they would remain on the outside, finding it necessary to shout in order to be heard. (They did shout sometimes and occasionally attempted to shake the structure in order to wake up the inhabitants, but academic women are generally not much given to picketing, sit-ins, forced entry, and riot.)

Figuring out the structure was not easy. It seems that for many committees there was a self-perpetuating group who nominated one another or their friends most of the time. Women demanded entrance to these groups and representation on the committees they controlled. Administrators and faculty members responded by appointing or nominating mainly "safe" (nonactivist) women to various committees. One popular appointee is a woman who in 1971 circulated among female faculty a statement declaring that sex discrimination was no problem on this campus because female faculty had never experienced any. Her effort met with little success. By the late 1970s women's names were more often found on committee lists, and some feminists even seem to have become respectable enough for committee work. The distribution is erratic, however. The elected committee that rounds up nominations for other elected committees has been all male for several years. The committees that pass on promotions to tenure in the physical and biological sciences are all male; those in the humanities and social sciences are twenty-five percent female. A few important appointed committees are equitably composed, but others are not. The net result suggests that campus women's power to maintain voice in campus affairs is not very secure.

The AFW also tried to have a direct effect on policy by creating a model affirmative action plan. Sixteen women worked for a year to produce a sophisticated, detailed blueprint for administrative activity and faculty response. This document was circulated among AFW members, administrators on this campus and others in the state system, and women throughout the country. Unanticipated demand for copies from outside the university was so great that the plan went through four printings by 1973. The campus AAO appreciatively acknowledged its receipt and mentioned that its suggestions would be attended to in several areas. The Committee on the Status of Women discussed the plan at one meeting. It may have been used as a reference or may have had some indirect effects after this, but as far as the AFW is aware the administration never looked at it a second time.

Some progress did occur on two other fronts, progress of a type that suggests how women might eventually achieve permanent voice. First, the major faculty committee for policy matters asked the activists (as well as many others) to discuss affirmative action problems with them. The committee members agreed that affirmative action was a faculty concern and established a faculty subcommittee to take up that concern permanently. This committee was structured and appointed with close attention to the nature of the organization of which it is a part and to the nature of the constituency it is intended to serve—those without other voice in faculty affairs. Most important, it answers to the faculty, not to the chancellor or the AAO. In spring 1976 this committee issued a report with recommendations for action that went far beyond the AAO's paper programs (although the AAO disputed this). Three years later the committee seems to have effected little permanent change; yet it has periods of outraged action that may eventually accomplish more than spot remedies for individual problems.

The second advance was the appointment of a committee charged with advising the health sciences vice-chancellor on policies to eliminate sex discrimination in all areas in that large center. Knowledgeable women (and even some activist women) from all ranks including nonprofessionals, were appointed to the committee, and the committee has maintained this kind of representation. It has been innovative and hard-working. As the nature and seriousness of the problems women employees face in this area became apparent, the committee's agenda expanded. Optimistic timetables gave way to pessimistic ones, but the committee's drive to accomplish its agenda also strengthened, and it continues to chalk up impressive accomplishments.

The lesson is clear: little is accomplished through minor changes in the traditional structure, such as appointing a few women to some committees. The existing structure has no channels for hearing suggestions from outside. Offering the administration a model for its policymaking was futile. What might be successful is the creation of new positions within that structure, positions that will serve to give women a longer lasting, more effective voice in policymaking.

The authors of the federal affirmative action guidelines seem to have been aware of the problem of achieving voice. The guidelines state that among the AAO's responsibilities is that of serving "as liaison between the contractor and minority organizations and community action groups concerned with employment opportunities of minorities and women. . . ."[7] But instead of liaison, the original AAO on this campus served to shield the university against activists. The AAO staff said that they were not interested in working with "self-appointed" groups. The AFW came to be routinely referred to as "those radical women," perhaps in hope of linking the group with the protesters who so disturbed campus peace in the past. For example, the AAO was quoted by a reporter as referring to the AFW as "a small group of people who are bitterly hostile to institutions . . . who want the institution brought down." The administration repeatedly said that the activist women were not representative of all women on campus, although there was no other organized group that might be more representative. It should be noted again that, although the AFW was organized by faculty, it involved all women on campus from the beginning. In fact, the AFW represented very well the powerless women who constituted the AAO's proper constituency.

The administration, however, professed to see that constituency as consisting of established faculty women who had no need for affirmative action. And therein lies the major problem: an underrepresented group cannot achieve voice when those designated as its legitimate representatives (by the administration) believe that there are no problems or that, if there are, only they and the administrators understand them. The administration and its female supporters refused to acknowledge substance to the criticism of concerned women. Instead they talked about "personality differences" that prevented them from working with AFW members. They decried the "fighting among women" that "hinders the ability of women to participate in academic life" and that is so "time-consuming . . . that little or no time can be spent in advancing the cause of women." Concerned campus women reacted to this kind of talk by ignoring it and by simply reemphasizing the substance of their criticism and the justice of their cause. The creation of the two committees described above suggests that steadfastly sticking to statement and restatement of substantive problems is probably the best tactic.

FAILURE THROUGH INAPPROPRIATE SOLUTIONS

The AAO did undertake many of the activities prescribed by federal affirmative action guidelines. These activities did not proceed along the lines suggested by the AFW model plan, however. Indeed, they seem to be not among the wisest that could be devised, judging by the results.

For example, most departments were required to formulate hiring goals for minorities and women. The AAO and the deans expedited the process by sending to department heads sets of memos with figures on the availability of minorities and women in each field and suggested goals. Departments were not involved in analyzing their own situations or formulating appropriate goals or devising ways to change hiring practices. With a few exceptions, most of them just read the memos (one assumes), filled out the goal statements with the figures provided by the AAO, and sent them back.

The lack of faculty involvement led to several problems. First, the AAO did not always understand a department's composition and so figured availability statistics from inadequate sources. If there was a choice, the lowest figure was used. The result was that goals were often set lower than departments, in good conscience, would have set them on their own.

Second, the authoritarian, top-down character of these memos is not conducive to educating academic men about how discrimination arises when they pursue traditional old boys' club methods. Even after many years, campus women were still discovering in chance conversations that even well-meaning men in their departments didn't know quite what affirmative action was or how to go about achieving it.

Third, one might count as evidence of effective pressure the worried or angry look that comes over the faces of department heads when affirmative action is mentioned. Yet there is no evidence that this pressure produced more commitment to equal opportunity for women than it produced annoyance, evasion, and excuses. There is likewise no evidence of adequate monitoring of hiring except in a few cases of departments whose lot it seemed to be to take more pressure than others. James C. Goodwin, in a brief piece with the same theme as this paper, suggests that the outcome of pressure to hire minorities and women can be a not-so-subtle discrediting of the justice of affirmative action.[8] Among his seven "games with affirmative action," Goodwin lists ways of making qualified minorities and women appear unavailable or unwilling to take open positions (for example, "single women don't want to come here and we can't get jobs for married women's husbands"), of making prospective female or minority candidates unwilling to take a position by letting them know that they're being hired only as tokens or only under pressure, or promoting reverse discrimination lawsuits by telling white men that they are the department's preferred candidates but that a minority or a woman has to be hired to satisfy affirmative action goals, and of generally assuming the appearance of good faith while managing to hire the really preferred white men.

A NONPROGRAM FOR AFFIRMATIVE ACTION

The first HEW team visited this campus in 1970. It found the existing affirmative action plan for the campus (dated April 1970) to be inadequate. In spite of a signed agreement with HEW, it was not until March 1974 that the university came up with a new, two-volume plan, not as a result of perceived legal, moral, or activist pressure but because the state regents directed it to bring the legally required programs into existence by that time. The new plan was not adequate, not by women's standards and not by the standards in the regents' written policy. It consisted of a collection of memos; inadequate, erroneous, and misleading statistics; and unverifiable claims of activity, plans, and programs for minorities and women. Members of the AFW had written critiques of various preexisting parts of the plan, but they appear to have been ignored.

This new plan was not submitted to HEW. When, in June 1975, the administration unexpectedly got a letter from HEW asking for an updated copy of the university's affirmative action plan, it apparently decided that the 1974 plan would not meet federal requirements, as subsequent events demonstrate.

The first letter was a simple request for a copy of the plan, but it was followed two days later by a letter saying that HEW had to review the compliance status of the campus in order to approve a federal grant of more than one million dollars. Since HEW had not been notified of pending grants soon enough to undertake the usual review procedure, however, it was giving the university a choice. The university could elect to submit its program and HEW would review it. If it met affirmative action guidelines, the university would get the money. If it did not meet the guidelines, the university would not have time to correct deficiencies by July 1 when the grants were to be awarded. Alternatively, the university could sign a forty-two-page agreement admitting noncompliance and stating that it was willing to write a program as directed in the agreement; then it would get its grant.

Members of the AAO's staff immediately set about "revising" the year-old plan, they said. They did not finish until the early morning hours of 30 June. The revised plan consisted of sixteen volumes, including twelve volumes of hastily run computer printouts of data on minority and female employees, two volumes of narrative and summary, and two volumes of memos to deans and departments that had been sent out over the years to instruct the faculty in affirmative action. All this was sent to HEW on 1 July. Although some of the material was newly written, this plan was not much of an improvement over the 1974 version; it was just fatter.

While this feverish activity was going on, the chancellor, along with officials from fourteen other universities who were unwilling to sign or submit their plans or who could not renegotiate their contract amounts or dates, met with the HEW secretary in Washington. The whole thing, they said, was outrageous, illegal, and inequitable. Secretary Caspar W. Weinberger agreed to work out a substitute agreement that was softer and shorter. The result was a three-page document that sounded firm but did not require the signatories to admit much. It did, however, request them to do what the original document called for: write up a program along specific lines. Officials from thirteen universities signed this new agreement. The representative of this campus was not among them. Why not? The chancellor was reported as having said, "It might commit [the university] farther than it wants to go in affirmative action."

The university got an extension until July 21 from the federal agency that was to award the large contract. HEW's regional office was supposed to decide whether the new plan was acceptable, but that office told the AFW that the final decision was to be made higher up. (Later a campus lawyer told a group of law students that, when a contract was held up, representatives of national higher education organizations in Washington go to the Washington higher-ups and persuade them to get the regional office "back on track"—apparently meaning to abandon enforcement efforts.) Representatives of the AFW and minority groups were told by HEW that it would review criticism of the program. But it was clear that such a review would be meaningless because these groups had no formal voice in the final decision.

Officially approved in July, the program seemed highly unlikely to improve the status of women and minorities on campus in the near future. It was deficient in meeting several federal guidelines, and many of its claims were unsubstantiated. In spite of HEW's claims that it investigated and resolved all complaints during the course of a compliance review, it ignored the broad-based complaint that the AFW filed in April 1974. But HEW came out of the confrontation looking as if it had gotten tough with the universities and thus perhaps hoped to quiet some of its loud-voiced critics and to gain an advantage in a legal action that a coalition of civil rights groups had taken against them. The university emerged from the conflict looking as if it had stood up to federal meddling into the meritocracy and shown the true morality of its position as well. But both parties had neglected minorities and women, who had no voice, no standing, and no power.

In late 1977 something changed rather quietly in HEW, probably as a result of an out-of-court settlement of the case brought by civil rights and women's groups charging HEW with nonenforcement of the law. The staff of HEW's Office of Civil Rights increased, policies changed, and perhaps the force of affirmative action regulations was unchained. HEW teams made site visits to several large universities, found them in substantial violation of Executive Order 11246, and produced lengthy agreements meant to force compliance with the guidelines. Officials of this university were among those who signed an agreement to remedy many of the problems mentioned in this paper: salaries, hiring, promotion, work-force analysis, monitoring procedures, and so forth.

The first nine months of 1978 saw some substantial work on these matters. Then in September 1978, shortly before reorganization of equal opportunity enforcement took contract compliance responsibility from HEW to the Office of Federal Contract Compliance Programs (OFCCP) in the Department of Labor, the university received a letter from HEW saying that it was in full compliance with affirmative action requirements. This simply was not so, as this paper shows. Even the signed agreement was not fulfilled. (The nonfaculty, nonclerical work-force analysis had not even been started, and the salaries of those employees had not been analyzed.) The new chancellor's statements of commitment to affirmative action seemed sincere, but there also seemed to be an instant replay of the fade-out, of games with statistics, of administrative hearing loss, of inappropriate solutions, and of the writing of toothless programs. The facade of affirmative action was generally refurbished with appropriate publicity.

It is too soon to write the end of this chapter. The OFCCP has not yet faded out, but even seems to talk rather tough. The activists, who by and large disappeared for a while, have begun to make common cause again. The state system regents decided that the status of women in the system needed looking into and appointed a task force to do so. Cases are going to court, reporters are looking for stories to give us the publicity we need, and women and minorities on campus are showing renewed determination to do something about discrimination in higher education. If this paper has shown anything, it is that success doesn't follow from words on paper and good intentions. The women on this campus have a lot of work ahead of them.

NOTES

[1]See Ruth Bleier, "Women and the Wisconsin Experience," *College English*, 34 (1972), 100–06; Gertrude Ezorsky, "The Fight over University Women," *New York Times Magazine*, 16 May 1972, pp. 32–39; Bernice Sandler, "A Little Help from Our Government: WEAL and Contract Compliance," in *Academic Women on the Move*, ed. A. S. Rossi and A. Calderwood (New York: Russell Sage Foundation, 1973), pp. 439–62; Deborah Shapley, "University Women's Rights: Whose Feet Are Dragging?" *Science*, 14 Jan. 1972, pp. 151–54.

[2]Some cases of gross inequity were settled, as might be expected, in ways that did not satisfy the women involved. For example, two lecturers achieved the status of tenured instructor, with no chance for promotion, loss of the privilege of teaching advanced courses, and, in one case, a cut in pay.

[3]This paper concerns affirmative action for women. The problems of race and class discrimination are different in many respects, and elimination of all forms of bias in academia will require a variety of changes. I have come to believe, however, that when it comes to getting universities to comply with antidiscrimination laws, underrepresented groups share many problems and should pursue the same basic course.

[4]For a description of how academics avoid recognizing sexism in their world, see Judith Long Laws, "The Psychology of Tokenism: An Analysis," *Sex Roles*, 1 (1975), 51–68; Lora Liss, "Why Academic Women Do Not Revolt: Implications for Affirmative Action," *Sex Roles*, 1 (1975), 209–23; Joan Abramson, *The Invisible Woman: Discrimination in the Academic Profession* (San Francisco: Jossey-Bass, 1975); Rosabeth Moss Kanter, "Some Effects of Proportions on Group Life: Skewed Sex Ratios and Responses to Token Women," *American Journal of Sociology*, 82 (1977), 965–90.

[5]Jacqueline Macaulay, "The Revolving Door for Faculty Women in Higher Education," unpublished paper (1980). This very slow gain is comparable to other major universities, as national statistics show. See annual reports on "Salaries and Tenure of Full-Time Instructional Faculty," from the National Center for Education Statistics. Unfortunately these reports do not separate

expansion in predominantly female fields from gains made by women in male-dominated fields.

[6]This typology is adapted from Albert O. Hirshman, *Exit, Voice, and Loyalty* (Cambridge, Mass.: Harvard Univ. Press, 1971). Those who protested or worked to reform the system took "voice" and worked with the AFW. Others chose "exit"; they wished the AFW well but were unable, for lack of time or tenure, to join. Some chose "loyalty," even though they perceived a problem. They tried to work with the AAO, pursuing case-by-case resolution of problems. These women saw success in cases solved and in a few confrontations with sexism. They tended to agree with the AAO in defining the controversy as either a power struggle or a mere fight among women, rather than as a problem that involved substantive issues. They dismissed criticism as radical rhetoric directed at those who are supposedly realistic about working with the establishment. They seldom dealt directly with the issues. Many of these women have been rewarded by the establishment with high-status posts.

[7]Department of Labor, Revised Order 4, Section 60-1.22.

[8]James G. Goodwin, "Point of View: Playing Games with Affirmative Action," *Chronicle of Higher Education*, 28 Apr. 1975, p. 24. For other papers that deal with themes found in this paper, see Marilyn Gittell, "The Illusion of Affirmative Action," *Change*, Oct. 1976, pp. 39–43; Joan I. Roberts, "Creating a Facade of Change: Informal Mechanisms Used to Impede the Changing Status of Women in Academe" (Pittsburgh: KNOW Press, 1976).

[9]For these views see "Editorial," *Washington Post*, 25 June 1975.

A Network of One's Own

Karen Childers, Phyllis Rackin, Cynthia Secor, and Carol Tracy

Aside from screening out people who are not old boys, what does an old boy network do? Without using the phrase, Virginia Woolf sketched its essential characteristics: the accumulated resources, shared influence, and conferred self-confidence that eased men's way in academe and left Woolf asking why men drank wine and women water at their separate but unequal tables in the halls of Oxbridge.

Today one can argue that women, especially in American coeducational institutions with their written affirmative action pledges, might count on infiltrating the network at last and that there is no need for a network of our own. And yet, even when the exceptional woman is allowed in, there is still an unspoken agreement that the net will seal behind her and that no more of her kind will follow until they, too, can prove they can make it without support. We argue that we need a separate network now more than ever, in view of rising expectations still largely unmet; that psychological support may mean at least as much as initial qualifications in giving women the courage to try and the will to succeed; and that women's work not only is not done but may never be done. In short, it is quite possible that, before significant numbers of women can enter the male network on anything like equal terms, we shall need a network of our own that will intersect with a male network without losing its own identity or compromising its goals.

WEOUP (Women for Equal Opportunity at the University of Pennsylvania) might be described as a network in spite of itself. The dozen or so women faculty, staff, and students who came together to perform one or two tasks in 1970 acted as catalysts in a series of existing organizations and attended the birth of new ones until today several thousand women are linked to one another on Penn's large, male-dominated campus.

WEOUP's history suggests some guidelines for forming a network of our own or revitalizing one that may have faltered after defeat (or victory) in the early rounds of our battle for equality on college campuses.

What made our network work? The attitudes of those who started it and the mixture of skills and contacts they brought to it. A strategy of spreading along preexisting communication paths and fitting new goals into existing agendas of women in all walks of life. A concentration on *work* in projects where women met as achievers, learned new skills, and gained respect for one another and for themselves.

THE WOMEN

A few women of roughly like mind are enough to start a network. Note the word "roughly." It is essential to concentrate on the common ground rather than the fine points of difference among women or within feminism itself. We were all committed to the single goal of equality in campus life, but we did not strive for ideological purity on other issues. As a result we were not divided by differences of opinion on abortion, sexual preference, unionization, or life-style. Some of us were more radical than others (and made no secret of our militancy), but as we expanded we came to include a number of more conservative women, and we made alliances that were productive for all of us. WEOUP women are individually active in a variety of causes, but within our network we all work for the improvement of career and study opportunities for women, through research, through persuasion and negotiation, and through pressure up to and including nonviolent demonstration and legal suit. The few ground rules have to do with race (nothing we ask for women will be won at the expense of minorities); violence (it is usually counterproductive); and patience with those not yet with us (you don't have to scratch a woman to find a sister, because the system will scratch her soon enough; just keep building the first-aid fund).

WEOUP grew primarily out of a "one-shot" project. In November 1970 a dozen women who barely knew one another naively asked the university's new president for a meeting to discuss how soon the Michigan decision would be implemented at Penn. The president sent the women off to draft an affirmative action plan and report back in ten days. And he didn't like what they brought back.

The combination of their skills was largely accidental but nearly ideal for the series of roles they took from that time on. An effective network should include at least one strong theorist, one data analyst, one writer, one good speaker, one shrewd analyst of group behavior, one veteran secretary who knows who's who and hates him for it, and one invulnerable front woman—a tenured faculty member, a student, a faculty wife (in our case she was a secretary who was willing to be fired, if necessary).

WEOUP had more than one of each and some with multiple skills. A lawyer would have helped; later we hired several.

In addition to their professional or positional qualifications WEOUP founders had experience in local party politics (traditional and radical), campus governance, civil rights marches, antiwar protest, gay rights, and Girl Scout work. Small as the group was it had faculty, both tenured and untenured, from the sciences as well as the humanities; administrative staff were junior and senior; clerical workers were pro-union and anti-union; students were from undergraduate and graduate programs. Alumnae and faculty wives were not in the initial group but joined later.

The combination of skills and backgrounds meant that the women could do research, identify problems, propose solutions, write documents that included solid data as well as rhetoric, study opposition for weak spots, stage and negotiate demonstrations, raise and tend funds, tap informal influence sources, and understand "the system" in minute detail. Some of us still doubt that we can change the system from within, but we are all convinced that we must understand the system if we want to survive.

Those of our core group who were most experienced at working within the system made a point of staying in and of drawing other women in by nominating them for office and committee service. Though most who were in the system had got there through the support of male friends and mentors—and they wisely did not abandon such friendships—some changes in those relationships did take place. Instead of dwelling on their fear of losing a mentor by emerging as feminists, the women worked to convert male friends to whatever degree of feminism the men could be brought to embrace, thus creating additional sources of support for all women's advancement. This was harder in the beginning than it was after the national movement began to affect the wives and daughters of male colleagues, but it was abetted by our honest conviction that the brightest and ablest men are secure enough not to have to prop up their identities by suppressing women as a class. One woman who is especially effective in committee strategy advises women electing to work within the system to cultivate one or more issues besides feminism with which to be identified. Being the best informed on the budget or the most knowledgeable or courageous on faculty rights, academic freedom, open expression, minority needs, or other such issues leads to respect and to potential alliances and trade-offs that are essential for a woman who is alone or outnumbered on a committee.

THE NETWORK

You probably have the beginning of a network on your own campus already. Find out where the women are; don't wait for them to come to you. Make ad hoc connections where common goals can be found, but do not ask for total commitment to your cause as the price of your cooperation in getting specific jobs done.

Some of WEOUP's founders had met in a middle-of-the-road Women's Faculty Club that sponsored monthly luncheon lectures across disciplinary lines. The club sponsored a rudimentary survey on women's status that led to an official study by the university. There is also a Faculty Tea Club, where faculty wives indeed pour tea (and conduct orientation for new arrivals and sponsor baby-sitting coops for student parents). That group was beginning to look at part-time employment and reentry counseling. And other groups emerged. The mostly male administrative staff formed an assembly to improve their own status at the university; the A-3 (support) staff also set up an assembly to work on problems of low status and isolation among rank-and-file clerical workers; an old and respected organization of chief clerks grew concerned about health benefits. Each of these groups presented an opportunity for WEOUP members to make alliances. Some of our bedfellows were very strange indeed: we were as surprised as anyone when male administrators joined a WEOUP-based day-care coalition in lobbying for child care—but of course they had working wives. The A-3 Assembly as a whole felt its tenuous existence could not stand the strain of a feminist position, but individuals crossed back and forth between the two groups, and we backed their proposals on reclassification and promotion.

Our fundamental strategy was to stay in touch with other groups and help them when they needed us. We could organize an activist committee or subcommittee, for example, without attempting to alter the organization's main agenda. Most such committees stressed information and analysis of conditions affecting the rights and especially the salaries of the employee groups involved. This meant that the activist committee had something solid to report to the parent group and that its work led to the adoption of recommendations that favored some of our positions.

Another useful practice was to invite a representative of every organized employee group to any negotiating session where their concerns might be discussed, fully aware that the representative might prove conservative. At one of those sessions an administrator turned to a retired chief clerk for support and she gracefully gave it this way: "It's true what he says, you know," she said softly. "Things have changed. When I came here twenty years ago a woman could walk across the Green but was not allowed to sit down on the benches. We can sit down now." She couldn't have done more for the movement if she had set fire to the chair the man was sitting in.

You might say that was a consciousness-raising experience, and WEOUP has done a lot to raise consciousness—male as well as female—on our campus. But consciousness raising was never our immediate goal. Individual WEOUP women took part in asser-tiveness training, attended workshops and conferences, joined consciousness-raising groups on campus or in the city, but as a group we avoided probing one another's souls any more than was necessary to resolve personal problems when they came up. (And they do come up: the point is that they are neither the end of the world nor the end of a movement unless they are magnified by being made the new agenda of the organization—to the detriment of its real agenda.)

THE WORK

The real agenda is and must be to get a job done for women. A critical mass of women dedicated to working effectively to eradicate discrimination can attract other women primarily by succeeding, by publicizing their success, and by recruiting new women on the basis of their needs, their skills, and the tasks they can perform. Work made ties for all sorts of women. More important, it gave new volunteers who were philosophically committed an immediate place in what could otherwise have seemed a clique of women who had been through early wars together.

The intensive, almost round-the-clock work—on projects ranging from writing an affirmative action plan to running a major conference on women in the academic community—forged a series of bonds that proved nearly unbreakable. Working together on these and other projects, overeducated and underutilized women suddenly had a chance to grow through exposure to one another's skills. In November 1970 we began with no concept of the basic structure of the university, the uses of statistics, the division of labor, the management of work flow, the techniques of interviewing and sampling, the interpretation of body language, or the overall techniques of planning and scheduling. By December we were veterans at much of it, and by spring, when the giant conference took place, nonspeakers were ready to conduct workshops and talk to the press, and nonwriters were ready to dash off a polemic that was strategically right as well as colorfully written. We learned these things from one another. Later we learned from our scientist members to prepare data analyses, for we discovered that the university had a tendency to include in its statistics women long since retired, resigned, or dead.

Some women have gone on to administrative jobs and high campus offices on the basis of skills learned and refined in WEOUP projects. Your own work projects will be different from ours, but here is a sampling of projects that WEOUP as an organization or its individual members have initiated or supported since the day the president didn't like the affirmative action plan:

1. Formally organized itself (wrote bylaws, elected officers, conducted a membership drive, raised operating funds from members and nonmembers). Hired an attorney.
2. Made contact with EEOC and with the human relations commission of our state.
3. Successfully negotiated a position for itself as a review committee for administration proposals and policies on women (the relationship between HEW and EEOC helped strengthen our hand). Followed through by studying federal and state regulations and guidelines, sending critiques, and publishing comment in campus and outside press.
4. Helped set up a Penn Women's Studies Planners group to write and lobby for a proposal to start a program here (now flourishing).
5. Supported the Rackin case by raising funds, politicking, publicizing the case, and publishing the Rackin papers (confidential papers obtained during legal proceedings).
6. Coordinated a national conference on women's studies.
7. Staged a four-day sit-in after five women were raped in three days and our security director implied in public that rape is women's own fault.
8. Negotiated, out of the sit-in, a women's center as headquarters for all women's activities, with two staff members and operating funds paid by the university.
9. In the course of sit-in negotiations, chose routes for lighting, designed a campus bus route, structured a campus escort service, developed a job description for a women's safety specialist to be added to the campus police.
10. Served on search committees for the safety-specialist position and for numerous others; acted as a referral service for

administrative and academic offices seeking to diversify the makeup of search committees.

11. Held weekly meetings open to all women; presented full agendas and work opportunities for anyone who attended.
12. Worked on the day-care coalition that some members started (with the result that a center, with academic ties to our social work school, is now open to campus and community children).
13. In small teams, convinced high-level administrators to resolve specific women's grievances.
14. Helped write formal grievance procedures for faculty and for nonacademic staff; provided names for grievance panels of both.
15. Lobbied against unfair search committees that would not interview women; caused such groups to be disbanded.
16. Supported student nurses in their protest against the screening of a pornographic film entitled *Student Nurses*.
17. Worked with the administration to establish a committee on sexual harassment.
18. Opposed the administration's attempt to change affirmative action procedures without consulting women and minority representatives on campus.
19. Forged an alliance with the Black Faculty and Administrators organization to oppose the university's secrecy in preparing data for a federal compliance review by the Department of Labor.
20. Organized support for Roselyn Eisenberg, a woman scientist, in her suit against the faculty of the university for sex discrimination (a suit that ended, like the Rackin case, in a satisfactory settlement).
21. Held a major conference in October 1978 to review our eight-year history and assess women's status and needs for the 1980s.
22. Supported and repeatedly defended the authority of our women's security specialist (now president of WEOUP).
23. Supported a current grievant (a minority woman) in her effort to secure adequate laboratory space, a fair salary, and tolerable conditions of employment. WEOUP gathered and analyzed twenty years' employment data from her school, raised money for her lawyers, and presented her case to the central administration.

Note the verbs on this list: *organized, studied, coordinated, negotiated*. Except for *staged* (a sit-in) they are words that might be found in a report on how to run Bell Telephone for fun and profit. We deal in productivity and draw strength from the conviction that an increase in women's presence at our university is a legitimate product.

Some of the pitfalls we face are similar to those found in an expanding enterprise anywhere—overdependence on some members, lack of delegation, failure to keep up communications—and some are unique to the special problems of women's emergence in the society.

There are several problems you should watch for. Class consciousness and status games, already endemic to academic institutions, can lead women to work at cross purposes, for example. Encourage mixed work teams: faculty and student research techniques can add muscle to studies of clerical misclassification, and nonacademic working women have information, useful skills, and perspectives that can enhance faculty strategies. Look consciously for each constituency's angle in studies or conferences on day care, safety, Title VII, Title IX, and so on. Demands that include several classes are harder for an administration to reject.

Another problem occurs when cliques develop out of concentrated teamwork. But, while one team is working on a discrimination case, several others can be tackling related issues (grievance procedures, for example) or unrelated ones. Have small teams give progress reports to the entire group or to other teams. Involve new members in existing teams or let them start their own; call back the formerly involved when their special issues resurface. Most important, recombine membership on new projects: don't let the core dwindle to an overworked few who will soon feel as put upon as others feel shut out.

The pressure that will fall on the most active members creates another problem. Accurately or not these women will be accused of neglecting their work, diluting their scholarship with feminist studies, being uncooperative with male colleagues. Let no woman face this alone: the group must notice, give psychological encouragement and specific help (from analyzing work flow to proofreading grant applications), and work through the grapevine in behalf of the woman's reputation. Nor should the group shy away from challenging the competence and motives of her detractors. We have found a high correlation between incompetence and antifeminism among males; yet even women will fall into the trap of believing men's negative evaluations of women. Examine carefully the source of any criticism. With whom is the detractor comparing this woman scholar—Einstein, or the last male the department hired? Is the detractor really that good himself? Is he threatened by her? Is he out of date?

Sometimes a needed woman will leave the university or be pushed out. If she has no place to go, rally your contacts to find her one. Help with her résumé and references. Look for free-lance and consulting opportunities to tide her over. Know what the institution does for men in such positions and make an issue of what it must do for her. Negotiated termination settlements, challenges to unemployment compensation claims, and grace periods in benefits coverage are subject to manipulation in favor of males and against females on many campuses. Keep in touch with the woman who leaves and never let the institution forget what it lost—statistically and substantively—when it was inhospitable to a good woman. Point up the falsehood of an affirmative action pledge that claims to seek good women but can't keep the ones it has.

The coopting of leadership has never happened to us here (we know of no woman who has been that fully accepted by our male establishment), but it may be a pitfall to be reckoned with on some campuses. On ours the larger problem is attrition of women, whether feminists or not, as tenure tightens unevenly on the sexes and terminations increase in lower administrative ranks. A shift from teaching to administration has been a solution for some women, but we also know from the record that every available opening in the administration will be filled by white males unless women individually and as a group make an issue of affirmative action beforehand. When jobs are filled without an affirmative action search, as many still are, formal protest is essential.

The fatal mistake in building a network is to relax your vigilance: to fall idle or go static in your program or to concentrate so heavily on a single cause or project that others fall by the wayside. Keeping up the activity level means listening to the membership for new needs, reaching out for the skills and ideas of newcomers, giving every woman you can reach a place as giver or receiver (or both) of services that the network can provide. It takes conscious periodic review of goals and progress to make sure that you are still relating to the changing needs of women on your campus and making some headway in solving the problems they bring to light. Are you accumulating resources for women (information, expertise, money)? Are you sharing influence with other women? Are you conferring self-confidence on one another (both formal recognition and word-of-mouth praise on the grapevine)? Every year your university will pass certain milestones that trigger reexamination: the budget will be adopted, faculty appointments made, honorary degrees conferred, senate officers elected, committees chosen, new students admitted, financial aid awarded, curricular changes announced. WEOUP is strongest when its members ask pointedly and out loud at each of these milestones, "What does this mean for women?" We have some ready answers of our own if we don't like the answers we get.

Your university will also faithfully assist you by its blunders. A recent example shows how much blunders help. During the seventies WEOUP's direct action receded as the university established the women's center, the women's studies program, and the rape prevention program, lent its support to HERS (Higher Education Resource Services) Mid-Atlantic training programs, and installed official structures to deal with grievances, conduct salary and classification reviews, and monitor affirmative action. We began to work at a distance, to channel women toward official resources of redress and to give counsel on affirmative action policy and procedure primarily through one structure, the Equal Opportunity Council. The council mirrors some of WEOUP's grassroots depth and variety by including all schools and administrative units and by carrying academic and nonacademic agendas in a single body. When the Department of Labor initiated an audit, however, the university bypassed its own official Equal Opportunity Council and entrusted both data analysis and policy and procedural change to a team of administrators led by newcomers who took a hard-line position on information sharing and consensus building. To aggravate matters, while some administrators faithfully promised that no new affirmative action policies or procedures would be implemented until the affected group had an opportunity to comment on them, others blithely began installing such changes. We seemed to be back at square one: some individuals in the administration had apparently decided that they would work in secret, negotiate a new plan, install it, and keep those nuisances (the women and minorities) from slowing down the work.

But the work went very slowly indeed, and the Department of Labor did not accept the staff team's submissions. The administration still refused to let us see the plan, and they claimed that the only problem holding up its acceptance was disagreement with the Department of Labor over its format.

Once again WEOUP had to go public. It took more than a year to build up enough leverage to pry the plan loose. This was a no-stones-unturned process: a joint effort with the black faculty and administrators, campus press comment, and the serendipitous opportunity to tell a national newsmagazine that we couldn't say how Penn was doing on equal opportunity for women because the university was keeping the new affirmative action plan secret.

In the uproar over these events, WEOUP saw an increase in membership unequaled since the first two years after its founding. Some of the new members are professionals and scholars in the fields of labor, management, and systems analysis. Far from neutralizing

WEOUP's power, the administration has inadvertently recruited a new cadre of militant exponents of women's rights. A strengthened organization faced a dual change of leadership early in 1981: a new president of the university and a new one in the White House. In this changing environment, WEOUP is developing new strategies determined to defend the ground women have gained and equally determined to continue our progress toward equalization, with or without Washington's support. This year the veterans have seen new strengths arise to meet new threats; the network is working.

Further Reading

Abel, Emily. "Collective Protest and the Meritocracy: Faculty Women and Sex Discrimination Lawsuits." Unpub. paper. California State University, Long Beach, 1979.

Abramson, Joan. *The Invisible Woman: Discrimination in the Academic Profession*: San Francisco: Jossey-Bass, 1975.

———. *Old Boys—New Women: The Politics of Sex Discrimination*. New York: Praeger, 1979.

Berger, Margaret A. *Litigation on Behalf of Women: A Review for the Ford Foundation*. New York: Ford Foundation, 1980.

"Fact Sheet on Women in Higher Education." Washington, D.C.: Women's Equity Action League Educational and Legal Defense Fund, 1979.

Howard, Suzanne. *But We Will Persist: A Comparative Research Report on the Status of Women in Academe, 1970-76*. Washington, D.C.: American Association of University Women, 1978.

Working It Out: Twenty-three Women Writers, Scientists and Scholars Talk about Their Lives and Work. Ed. Pamela Daniels et al. New York: Pantheon, 1977.

Organizations to Write for Information

American Association of University Professors
One Dupont Circle
Washington, D.C. 20036

American Association of University Women
2401 Virginia Avenue, N.W.
Washington, D.C. 20037

Project on the Status and Education of Women
Association of American Colleges
1818 R Street, N.W.
Washington, D.C. 20009
 (202) 387-1300

The Project on the Status and Education of Women distributes free materials that identify and highlight issues and federal policies affecting women's status as students and employees. The materials include the newsletter and papers in the following categories: Title IX, other legal requirements (includes a chart on federal laws and regulations concerning sex discrimination in educational institutions), recruiting students and employees, minority women, and other papers on topics such as rape, sexual harassment, and women's centers.

Women's Equity Action League Educational and Legal Defense Fund
805 15th Street, N.W., Suite 822
Washington, D.C. 20005
 (202) 638-1961

Ask for the Higher Education Kit.